Opening *the* Door *to* Your Future

Keys to personal and professional success

Opening *the* Door *to* Your Future

Keys to personal and professional success

Lamont McLean

WHITAKER
HOUSE

OPENING THE DOOR TO YOUR FUTURE:
Keys to Personal and Professional Success

Lamont McLean Ministries
P. O. Box 8204
Cherry Hill, NJ 08002
www.lamontmcleanministries.com

ISBN: 978-0-88368-712-3
Printed in the United States of America
© 2007 by Lamont McLean

1030 Hunt Valley Circle
New Kensington, PA 15068
www.whitakerhouse.com

Library of Congress Cataloging-in-Publication Data
McLean, Lamont, 1955–
Opening the door to your future : keys to personal and professional success / Lamont McLean.
p.   cm.
Summary: "Lamont McLean draws on his background as a successful businessman and pastor to provide thirty keys that, when applied, can lead to lives of greater personal and professional success"—Provided by publisher.
ISBN 978-0-88368-712-3 (trade hardcover : alk. paper) 1. Success—Religious aspects—Christianity. I. Title.
BV4598.3.M435 2007
248.4—dc22   2007017354

1 2 3 4 5 6 7 8 9 10 11 12 **UJ** 15 14 13 12 11 10 09 08 07

Praise for
Opening the Door to Your Future

"Opening the Door to Your Future provides powerful nuggets of truth to get you on the fast track to victorious living. It reinforces our decision to be faithful despite constant warfare from the enemy. This book spoke to me on many levels and has helped me in my walk with God, as my desire is to reach the next level in victorious living."

—William "Tra" Thomas
Three-time NFL Pro-Bowl Tackle
Philadelphia Eagles

ACKNOWLEDGMENTS

I would like to acknowledge some very special people who have been instrumental in the completion of this book.

My heartfelt thanks to Phillip and Brenda Goudeaux, my spiritual father and mother, for direction, encouragement, and the inspiration to undertake this project.

Special thanks to Kenneth and Gloria Copeland, for your words of wisdom and guidance, which helped me complete this project.

I am grateful to Melanie Hemry for your faithful editorial assistance.

And, most of all, thanks to my beautiful wife, Connie, for taking this walk of faith with me. Your unwavering love and dedication have helped to bring out the best in me. I love you.

—Lamont McLean

CONTENTS

PREFACE

God gives His children the very best that He has to offer—Jesus. With the Spirit of the Lord dwelling within, no people on earth should outshine Christians. Through God's spirit of excellence, believers should lead the way in every field. The world should be looking to Christians for inspiration in art, science, literature, and medicine. We should be the best businessmen, the best parents, and the best civic leaders that the world has to offer.

Yet like a caboose tacked on to the end of a fast-moving train, Christians bring up the rear far too often. Overlooked, outshined, and passed by, many Christians suffer from a critical case of low self-esteem and a chronic fear of failure.

Recognizing a gap between the promises within the Word of God and the reality of how many Christians function in the world today, I have tried to tackle the problem with the same methodical approach I used in solving the business dilemmas of my past. While ministering to the broken lives of my church members, I studied the keys of both personal and professional success. Then, applying the Word of God, I taught my flock how to close that gap and find the faith to be the best that God has to offer.

This book is designed to help you identify the missing keys to success in your life. It will help you to mix your faith and

11

belief system with a little positive action in a way that will cata-
pult you out of powerless living and into your divine destiny.

All it takes is a small key to unlock the largest door. Likewise, each key in the Christian's faith is crucial to unlock what
blocks your path so you can enter into the presence of God. In
short, using these simple keys to success will give you faith to
be the best at whatever you set out to accomplish.

The principles in this book are not untried. Before teaching them to members of my church, I discovered them for
myself. Using them, I was able to overcome a life-long speech
impediment and dead-end career to become a successful
entrepreneur and pastor.

Opening the Door to Your Future is designed for frustrated
people living powerless lives. It is for those who find themselves
falling into the same traps over and over again. Through my
in-depth study of the Bible and uncompromising stand on
applying biblical principles to everyday problems, I have iden-
tified several crucial keys to a successful life.

Each chapter is a compelling life principle, supported by
Scripture, which will allow you to check your own spiritual
pulse. The end of each chapter includes a Faith Key—questions for reflection, suggestions for practical application—as
well as a prayer to help you reset your spiritual course.

Key #1

GREAT EXPECTATIONS

Your Success in Life Will
Never Exceed Your Expectations

You have been chosen by God to live in one of the greatest times in the history of the world. God has given you His Spirit, His name, His authority, and His power. Perhaps you already love the Lord and have committed your life to Him. At church, under the corporate anointing, you feel so full of the glory of God you could dance in the aisles.

Then you go home. The glory fades when you walk in and face the mountains of dirty laundry, a feverish baby, and sullen teenagers. The next morning, you go to work and wonder if you'll ever make any headway up the corporate ladder. Sure, you receive cost-of-living raises, but someone else always gets the big promotions. Your back aches, your head aches, and—worst of all—if a coworker is facing a crisis and asking for prayer, you know without a doubt that you have nothing left within you to give him or her.

In short, you're living a powerless life.

I believe that we, the body of Christ, are living well below our position in the "God Class." God has given us everything we need to live victorious lives, but when it comes to walking out that victory day by day, there's something missing.

This book is designed to help you to identify the keys to your victorious life and to unlock the door leading to faith, a belief system, and the positive action that will move you out of powerless living and into your divine destiny.

Each key is crucial to pull you out of the pits and hoist you up to the high places with God. In short, using the right key will open the door to your victorious life and will give you faith to be the best at whatever you set yourself to accomplish.

By the time you finish this book, you will no longer struggle to climb the corporate ladder. You'll have the faith to own the ladder.

> God has given us everything we need to live victorious lives.

I encourage you not simply to read this book, but to digest it. Allow the principles to take root in your heart. Put feet to your faith by making the necessary changes to step out of your own limitations and into the limitless power of God.

I know you've been riding the boat of your Christian life white-knuckled, powerless to do more than hold on. But as you discover the keys to personal and professional success, you'll finally be able to let go and step out of the boat. Like Peter did two thousand years ago, step out of your comfort zone, lift your eyes to Jesus, and walk on water.

"What if I sink?" you ask. If you feel yourself sinking, put your hand in Jesus' hand. He will lift you up. Then pull this book off the shelf and read it again. Figure out what key you are missing. Make your corrections and step into the most exhilarating life you can imagine.

You're in the "God Class"—expect miracles.

Let this message sink into the ears of anyone who listens to what the Spirit is saying to the churches: *"to everyone who is victorious, I will give fruit from the Tree of Life in the Paradise of God"* (Revelation 2:7 TLB).

RAISING YOUR EXPECTATIONS

I still recall the excitement that coursed through me as a new believer when I gave my life to the Lord Jesus. The zeal of the Lord filled me, and I was vitally aware that I was a new creation. Old things had passed away. I knew that anything was possible because the Lord was in me!

"Now, don't expect too much!" mature believers warned me. I guess I matured rapidly, because it wasn't long before I didn't expect much.

hard for christians darkside of the christ

I suspect that, like me, you're tired of falling short of God's best. God's Word tells us that we can do all things through Christ who strengthens us. (See Philippians 4:13.) But for the most part, the body of Christ doesn't have a can-do attitude. We don't have the mind of Christ when we "have not," "can't get," and "always need."

God's Word says that He will *"supply all your needs according to His riches in glory"* (Philippians 4:19). Is the Word of God contradicting your lifestyle? If so, you need to discover the keys that will open the door to personal and professional success.

But without faith it is impossible to please Him, for he who comes to God must believe that He is, and that He is a

15

rewarder of those who diligently seek Him.

(Hebrews 11:6)

One of those keys is your expectations. Religion has attempted to stomp out our expectations in God. But the Bible tells us that in order to please God, we must believe that He will reward us for seeking Him. In other words, having high expectations is a prerequisite to living victoriously!

BLESSED WITH THE BEST

Take a fresh look at John 3:16 without stumbling over its familiarity:

For God so loved the world that He gave His only begotten Son, that whoever believes in Him should not perish but have everlasting life.

According to this Scripture, God gave us His only Son. In other words, He gave us the best that He had. He could have reached back and grabbed anything from heaven. He could have given us an angel. He has lots of angels and certainly could have spared one.

But God didn't send an angel to redeem mankind. He blessed us with the greatest gift He had to offer—His only Son. Clearly, God decided to bless us with His best. And He didn't bless us from earth's resources, but from the very best that heaven had to offer.

There's only one problem—we're not used to the best. We're used to compromise. We'll settle for whatever we can get. Some of you will settle for average. Many of you will settle for below average. Sadly, others of you will settle for failure. But I want you to understand that compromise didn't come to

16

you from God. He didn't give you the gift of compromise. God gave you His best when He gave you Jesus.

That would have been enough, but the best didn't stop there. Jesus said and did the same things that His Father said and did. *"I do nothing of Myself; but as My Father taught Me, I speak these things"* (John 8:28). Jesus saw His father give His best, and Jesus did the same thing.

In John 14:16–17, Jesus said,

> *I will pray the Father, and He will give you another Helper, that He may abide with you forever; the Spirit of truth, whom the world cannot receive, because it neither sees Him nor knows Him; but you know Him, for He dwells with you and will be in you.*

Obviously, Jesus gave His very best when He gave the Holy Spirit. That means the Spirit of God is in you. What I want you to understand is that you are filled with the greatness of God.

Therefore, it stands to reason that what you give should be the best.

PROGRAMMED FOR GREATNESS

I know that this is contrary to your experience. I understand that it's contrary to your circumstances. It may be contrary to what you've heard. But the Word of God says that you are programmed to be the best. It's in your spiritual DNA! And if you think about it for a moment, you'll recognize that it's been in you since you were born again.

Let me ask you this. Have you ever wanted to be an average parent? Have you ever wanted to be an average spouse? No, because that's not the way you were created. I can honestly say I don't want to be an average father. I don't want to be an average pastor. I want to be the best, and that doesn't come from a spirit of pride, it comes from the Spirit of God!

The problem lies in the fact that while God programmed you for greatness, the world has been hard at work trying to reprogram you for mediocrity. The world wants to shut you up and make you sit in your corner. But children of God should be the best at everything they set their hands to do. When promotions come up, you should be at the top of the list.

You need to get the mind-set that you're the best—not average! Average is equal parts of good and bad. Yet most people think,

I'm just your good old average Christian.

I'm going to struggle in this life, but when I get to the other side, God will bless me.

God already gave you His best! I'm weary of doormat Christians who won't stand up for who they really are. The body of Christ has poor self-esteem! It's not about who we are, but who He is in us!

> *"No weapon formed against you shall prosper, and every tongue which rises against you in judgment you shall condemn. This is the heritage of the servants of the LORD, and their righteousness is from Me," says the LORD.*
>
> (Isaiah 54:17)

The Bible tells us that no weapon formed against us will prosper. It tells us that the devil has been defeated and is under our feet. It tells us that we can do all things through Christ who strengthens us. Therefore, if no weapon formed against you can prosper, your enemy has been defeated, and you can do all things through Christ—I'd say God is telling you that you're the best.

Being the best means that there is no obstacle you cannot overcome. If an obstacle can overcome you, then you're certainly not the best. If a situation or a circumstance can overcome you, the Greater One isn't living freely in you.

A SPIRIT OF EXCELLENCE

The Bible says that Daniel had a spirit of excellence because the Spirit of the Holy God was in him. (See Daniel 5:11–12.) Daniel was a great man of God. A Hebrew sold into slavery, he was the least of the least in Babylonian captivity. Yet even in his circumstances, Daniel refused to give less than his best. As a consequence, God promoted him until he had great favor with the king.

> Being the best means that there is no obstacle you cannot overcome.

Think about your circumstances today. No doubt you're facing difficulties, but are you a slave in a foreign country? Are you facing great religious persecution? Daniel was. He was ordered by a royal decree to bow down and worship the king or be thrown in a lion's den. Daniel could have easily gotten a "woe-is-me" attitude. "What's the point in serving God? I'm a slave about to be torn apart by hungry lions for my faith."

Here's the excellence of Daniel. He continued to give his very best. And he refused to compromise. He'd rather be torn apart by lions than bow.

> *Now when Daniel knew that the writing was signed, he went home. And in his upper room, with his windows open toward Jerusalem, he knelt down on his knees three times that day, and prayed and gave thanks before his God, as was his custom since early days.* (Daniel 6:10)

19

According to the Bible, the king wasn't able to sleep the night after Daniel had been thrown in the lion's den. He refused food or comfort. Early the next morning, the king rose and went to the den calling,

Daniel, servant of the living God, has your God, whom you serve continually, been able to deliver you from the lions?
(Daniel 6:20)

Then Daniel said to the king,

O king, live forever! My God sent His angel and shut the lions' mouths, so that they have not hurt me, because I was found innocent before Him; and also, O king, I have done no wrong before you. (verses 21–22)

Notice the impression that David's spirit of excellence made on the pagan king.

Then King Darius wrote: To all peoples, nations, and languages that dwell in all the earth: Peace be multiplied to you. I make a decree that in every dominion of my kingdom men must tremble and fear before the God of Daniel. For He is the living God, and steadfast forever; His kingdom is the one which shall not be destroyed, and His dominion shall endure to the end. He delivers and rescues, and He works signs and wonders in heaven and on earth, who has delivered Daniel from the power of the lions. (verses 25–27)

Daniel's example made a heathen king turn to the God of the universe. It caused a whole kingdom to bow before the Holy One of Israel. If you are born again, the same spirit of excellence that resided within Daniel resides in you.

God has great expectations for you.

Don't you think it's time you had them for yourself?

CONFESSION:

Father, forgive me for setting my expectations so low. Forgive me for doubting that I could be the best when You—*the Best of the best*—live in me. You gave Your best, Jesus, for me. With Your help I will give my best for You. Please cause my expectations to rise and match Your plan for my life. I ask this in Jesus' name. Amen.

FAITH KEY #1—GREAT EXPECTATIONS

Having high expectations is a prerequisite to personal and professional success. Read the following Scripture and ask yourself this question: What do you honestly expect from the God of the Universe dwelling in you?

If you want to know what God wants you to do, ask him, and he will gladly tell you, for he is always ready to give a bountiful supply of wisdom to all who ask him; he will not resent it. But when you ask him, be sure that you really expect him to tell you, for a doubtful mind will be as unsettled as a wave of the sea that is driven and tossed by the wind; and every decision you then make will be uncertain, as you turn first this way, and then that. If you don't ask with faith, don't expect the Lord to give you any solid answer.

(James 1:5–7 TLB)

GIVE THE BEST

God gave His best when He gave you Jesus. How have you compromised the Best that is in you—at work, in your relationships, in your finances, and in your faith? Write down your

21

answers and make each of them a matter of prayer, releasing your faith for change.

Don't worry if your past is full of compromise and rebellion. God, your heavenly Father, is always ready for His children to turn back toward Him, inheriting all the blessing and provision that comes with being a child of the King. Read God's welcome to the return of every prodigal son and daughter:

> *And he arose and came to his father. But when he was still a great way off, his father saw him and had compassion, and ran and fell on his neck and kissed him. And the son said to him, "Father, I have sinned against heaven and in your sight, and am no longer worthy to be called your son." But the father said to his servants, "Bring out the best robe and put it on him, and put a ring on his hand and sandals on his feet. And bring the fatted calf here and kill it, and let us eat and be merry."* (Luke 15:20–23)

Key #2

DON'T BUY THE LIE

The Truth Will Set You Free

Wouldn't you agree that everyone desires a spirit of excellence? It's hard to imagine anyone wanting mediocrity. So why aren't all believers doing all things through Christ who strengthens them?

Because many don't believe they can!

Isn't that a shame? God blessed you with His best, but when He asks you to do exploits in His name you say, "I can't." The world has programmed you to feel that you can't be the best. The world is lying to you, and you've bought into it.

The word *best* means "to the utmost." Salvation is the perfect example of God giving His utmost. Everything that God has is wrapped up in salvation. In other words, when you receive salvation, you have it all. You have the best. You have the utmost from God.

The problem lies in the fact that many never realize this. They think, *Oh, I just accepted Jesus.*

23

No! That's where you're limiting God. Salvation isn't just *accepting* Jesus, it's *receiving* Jesus. It is possible to accept Jesus as Savior, but never receive Him as Lord and Master over all your life.

Think about that.

If you don't receive Him, you don't have the Greater One operating in your life the way He should be. Therefore, you buy the lie that you're not good enough. The devil is desperate that you stay deceived about who you are in Christ Jesus. He knows, as does all of heaven, that once you receive the Eternal One as Lord and Master over all your life, you will never bow down to anyone, anything—any demon, any person, any organization, or any government. Like Daniel, your knee will bow only to God.

THE ONLY TRICK

Satan is terrified that you will find out who you are in Christ Jesus. He is terrified that you will release the God of glory that's inside you. He does not want more Daniels running around, and he certainly doesn't want Jesus set loose in you! So how does he stop you? The same way he stopped Eve in the garden of Eden—through deception. It's still the only trick up his sleeve.

In the garden, God told Adam that he could eat of any tree except the Tree of Knowledge of Good and Evil. He warned that if Adam ate of this tree, he would die. The fall of the human race came about because Satan lied and told Eve, *"You will not surely die"* (Genesis 3:4).

God said, "You will die." (See Genesis 3:3.)

Satan said, "You will not die." (See verse 4.)

24

Eve had a choice: believe God, or believe Satan. She could walk through door number one or door number two. Door number one offered eternal bliss in the garden of God. Door number two offered spiritual death, expulsion from the garden, and a lifetime of hard labor. She was told that there was life behind one door and death behind the other. It should have been a slam-dunk, except that the devil whispered, in effect, "What if death isn't behind door number two?"

That lie was all he had! He didn't have the ability to create anything—except an illusion. Eve fell for it. She rolled the dice and gambled. Most of us shake our heads, incredulous that Eve could make such a blunder.

Let's be honest for a moment. How often have you made the same mistake? What if this choice (alcohol, drugs, sexual promiscuity, lying, cheating, adultery, gossip, backbiting, prayerlessness, financial irresponsibility) really doesn't lead to death?

This is the lie above all lies, and it's still being perpetrated millennia later. Scripture says, *"He who is in you is greater than he who is in the world"* (1 John 4:4).

To which the devil replies, "God isn't powerful in you."

You believe the lie.

Jesus said, *"He who believes in Me, the works that I do he will do also; and greater works than these he will do, because I go to My Father"* (John 14:12).

Satan laughs and whispers, "You will not."

You believe you can't.

God put the very best inside you—Himself. Yet you aren't working out the salvation that God put in you because every day you wake up and buy the lie that you're powerless.

*If the Good News we preach is hidden to anyone, it is hidden
from the one who is on the road to eternal death. Satan, who
is the god of this evil world, has made him blind, unable to
see the glorious light of the Gospel that is shining upon him,
or to understand the amazing message we preach about the
glory of Christ, who is God.* (2 Corinthians 4:3–4 TLB)

The Bible makes it clear that Satan has blinded the minds
of those who are lost. They're like people lost in a fog, thinking they're headed one direction when they're really about to
step off a cliff into eternity. No one who sees clearly would willingly walk into hell.

But here's what most Christians fail to realize: just
because you got saved doesn't mean the devil is going to
stop trying to blind you to the things of God. That's why the Bible tells you
to renew your mind. (See Romans 12:2.)

> Just because you got saved doesn't mean the devil will stop trying to blind you to the things of God.

While I don't believe that a Christian can be possessed by the devil,
the Bible makes it clear that he wants
to have you. Jesus told Peter that the
devil wanted to "sift him as wheat."
Guess what happened? Peter vowed to join Jesus in prison and
in death. (See Luke 22:31, 33.)

Jesus said, *"I tell you, Peter, the rooster shall not crow this day
before you will deny three times that you know Me"* (verse 34).

Earlier, Peter had declared to Jesus, "You're not going to
die." (See Matthew 16:22.)

Jesus replied, *"Get behind Me, Satan!"* (verse 23). At that
moment, Satan had Peter.

"Wait a minute!" you might say. "Peter was a great man of God!"

He would become a great man of God, but at that particular moment he was tempting Jesus to disobey the plan of God for His life.

In 2 Corinthians, Paul wrote,

*But I fear, lest somehow, as the serpent deceived Eve by his craftiness, **so your minds may be corrupted** from the simplicity that is in Christ.*

(2 Corinthians 11:3, emphasis added)

Who was Paul talking to? Christians of the church at Corinth! Paul warned Christians that Satan wanted to deceive them the same way he deceived Eve.

Clearly, the devil can beguile a Christian. Think about it. Eve lost her mind for a moment. Nobody in their right mind would believe the devil over God. She must have had a momentary lapse into insanity.

The devil plays mind games. Most believers are blind to his tactics. Your victory today, tomorrow, and every day for the rest of your life depends on whether or not you win the war against Satan. Everything depends on whether or not you buy the lie.

For whatever is born of God overcomes the world. And this is the victory that has overcome the world; our faith.

(1 John 5:4)

YOU HAVE THE ANSWER

The answer to your problem is not the church. You are looking all around trying to find the key to unlock your victorious life when God has already provided the solution. What activates this solution? Your faith.

Most people don't realize that faith isn't mental assent. Believing something with your head won't bring your breakthrough. Faith is a spiritual force that grows when the Word of God is planted and nurtured in your heart.

It is your faith in God that draws the best out of you. Faith comes from God; therefore, faith always reaches for the best. Faith doesn't reach for average. It doesn't reach for compromise.

God told Abraham that his descendents would be as many as the stars in the sky. Yet at one hundred years of age, Abraham was a dried up old prune of a man. Despite all odds, he still believed what God had promised. Faith—his faith—reached inside his body, which was as good as dead, and pulled out nations.

It was faith that went into Moses, a stuttering outcast from Egypt, and pulled out a deliverer. It was faith that reached into David, a sixteen-year-old shepherd, and pulled out a giant killer and king. It was faith that reached into Mary, a virgin girl from the sticks, and pulled out the King of Kings and Lord of Lords.

The same power that raised Jesus from the dead resides in you.

Stop the insanity.

Stop buying the lie.

CONFESSION:

Father, I ask that You forgive me for buying into lies. I repent for buying the lie that I should compromise my faith. I repent for buying the lie that You are not powerful enough to do exploits through me. I repent for buying the lie that my weakness is greater than Your power. I repent for buying the lie that the best is not in me. I want to stop the insanity. Please help me to renew my mind daily. Help me to remember that it's not about me, but it's about You. Help me have great expectations for victorious living. Help me win the battle for my mind—every moment of every day. Amen.

FAITH KEY #2—
RECEIVE THE LORD AND MASTER

If you are born again, you have accepted Jesus as your Savior. But have you received Him as Lord and Master over all your life? Is He Lord and Master of your destiny? Is He Lord and Master of your relationships? Is He Lord and Master of your time? Is He Lord and Master of your finances? Is He Lord and Master of your thoughts?

What areas of your life have you withheld from Him?

Are you willing to receive Him?

He came to His own, and His own did not receive Him.
(John 1:11)

REFUSE TO BUY THE LIE

Jesus said that the devil is the father of lies, and no truth is in him. The devil's weapon is lies, and that is what he hurls at you day and night. You will never live a victorious life until you take every thought captive and refuse to buy his lies.

Look back over the intersections of your life to date. Make a quick review of your decisions and choices—the things you did and those you didn't do. In light of the Bible, write down the lies you have believed about God and yourself that have worked to sabotage your victorious life.

Heed the warning that Jesus gave to the Pharisees—that if we believe the lies long enough, we will no longer recognzie truth when we hear it:

> *For you are the children of your father the devil and you love to do the evil things he does. He was a murderer from the beginning and a hater of truth—there is not an iota of truth in him. When he lies, it is perfectly normal; for he is the father of liars. And so when I tell the truth, you just naturally don't believe it! Which of you can truthfully accuse me of one single sin? (No one!) And since I am telling you the truth, why don't you believe me? Anyone whose Father is God listens gladly to the words of God. Since you don't, it proves you aren't his children.* (John 8:44–47 TLB)

Key #3

THE ONE PERCENT

Dare to Compare

The world population fluctuates moment by moment. Somewhere, someone dies, and someone else is born. At the time of this publication, the U.S. Census Bureau estimates the world population at 6,583,677,717. That's a lot of people. But did you know that only an estimated 1 percent of that total will actually have a meaningful influence on the rest of the world?

In the year 2000, the richest 1 percent of adults owned 40 percent of the world's total assets.[1]

According to Jackie Huba and Ben McConnell, coauthors of *Citizen Marketers: When People Are the Message*, advertisers recognize that 1 percent of the U.S. are the real influencers of the rest of the country. "They're what we call the 'One Percenters,' the people who live at the edges and are different than 99

---

[1] Davies, J, Sandstrom, S., Shorrocks, A., and Wolff, E. 2006. *The World Distribution of Household Wealth*. http://www.wider.unu.edu/research/2006-2007/2006-2007-1/wider-wdhw-launch-5-12-2006/wider-wdhw-report-5-12-2006.pdf

percent of the world....The One Percenters often become the influencers of American culture."[2]

Most likely, you are not one of them.

But you should be.

That's a troubling thought, isn't it? I suspect it makes you uncomfortable, and you really don't believe that it's true. That's because you don't know, as yet, who you are. If you are born again, you are of God.

BECOMING NEW

In one of his letters to the church at Corinth, Paul wrote,

Therefore if any man be in Christ, he is a new creature: old things are passed away; behold, all things are become new.
(2 Corinthians 5:17 KJV)

I know it's a familiar Scripture, but do you really believe it? Paul did. It's obvious by his life. Known as Saul, he was a Hebrew, an Israelite, a descendent of Abraham, and a great Jewish scholar. He imprisoned and beat those in every synagogue who believed in Jesus. He gave his consent to the men who murdered Stephen, holding their coats while they stoned him. (See Acts 22:19–20.)

Yet when Paul received Jesus, he became a new creature. He preached the gospel at great peril. He was imprisoned, received thirty-nine lashes on five different occasions, was beaten with rods, stoned, shipwrecked three times, and was adrift in the open sea all of one night and the next day. (See 2 Corinthians 11:23.) He traveled many weary miles to preach the

[2] Kawasaki, G. 2006. *The "One Percenters."* http://www.business-opportunities.biz/2006/12/09/the-one-percenters.

gospel. He was the great apostle who oversaw all the churches and wrote a large portion of the New Testament.

Saul, the religious fanatic determined to drive Christianity out of the world, met Jesus, and became such a new creature that he was transformed into Paul, willing to suffer and die for the sake of the gospel. Two thousand years later, none of us is untouched by his life and his teaching.

A NEW MIND

So let me ask you: are you a new creature?

If you are not, then you aren't really born again. I don't mean to be rude, but the Bible is very clear on this subject. New birth always forms a new creature. But I must warn you, when you became a new creature, your mind wasn't included in the deal. That's why Paul also wrote,

> The strongholds that must be pulled down are in your mind.

*For the weapons of our warfare are not carnal but mighty in God for **pulling down strongholds,** casting down arguments and every high thing that exalts itself against the knowledge of God, **bringing every thought into captivity to the obedience of Christ.***
(2 Corinthians 10:4–5, emphasis added)

According to this Scripture, the strongholds that must be pulled down are in your mind, and to do that you must bring every thought into captivity.

Your new man was designed to be a part of the 1 percent. And to fulfill that design you must renew your mind to who you are as a new creature in Christ Jesus.

33

Think about it for a moment.

You are of God, and no one is greater than God. The church—made up of all believers—is the body of Christ. The Bible says that Jesus is the ruler over all. It says that He is the first and last. (See Revelation 1:8.) He surpasses the one percent!

So, who does that make you?

It makes you, like Paul, one of the most influential people on the planet. But to take your place, you're going to have to change the way you think.

Dear young friends, you belong to God and have already won your fight with those who are against Christ because there is someone in your hearts who is stronger than any evil teacher in this wicked world. (1 John 4:4 TLB)

RE-CREATED IN CHRIST

We believers tend to repeat the same religious phrases all the time:

"I am a new creature in Christ!"

"Old things have passed away!"

"Behold all things have become new!"

While there is nothing wrong with those confessions, it's time to stop and listen to the words. Translated from the Greek, the Bible says that you are a new creature. It means that God created you all over again. But this time He didn't use your parts. He used the same ingredients, the same components, and the same parts He used when He sent Jesus to earth. But this time, He re-created you with His Word.

You have been empowered with the same abilities and the same faith that Jesus had. I know it's an astounding thought, because you don't look any different. Chances are you don't feel any different. An old car that's been supercharged with a powerful new engine doesn't look or feel any different either. At least, not until you start it.

You've been walking around feeling powerless because you don't understand the new equipment that God installed within you. You have to start the engine by faith. It will kick in. If you'll look under the hood with the eyes of faith, you'll discover that God has given you everything you need to be an influencer for the kingdom—part of the 1 percent.

KING OF THE COURT

It may help you to think about some of those who are unquestionably in the 1 percent of the world's system. For instance, if I asked you who was among the 1 percent in basketball, Michael Jordan would head the list. Why is he still considered among the best who ever played? It's because he outwitted all his opponents.

God created Michael Jordan with everything he needed to be among the 1 percent in basketball. But Michael didn't just wake up one morning and expect success to be handed to him. Although he had the right equipment, he had to prove his position. That meant staying after practice and spending hour after hour making sure he mastered the fundamentals. It meant never giving up. It meant believing he was the best before anyone else on earth figured it out.

That's where many Christians miss it. They don't want to believe it until they see it—and that's not faith! In addition, they don't want to pay the price of becoming a winner.

God has given you the equipment to join the 1 percent, as surely as He gave it to Michael Jordan. He is waiting to see what you'll do with it.

KING OF THE RING

God was the only one who knew He had put "the right stuff" inside a scrawny, flyweight boxer from Louisville, Kentucky, in 1954. The only one, that is, except for Cassius Clay himself. God didn't bring Cassius into the world with the physique of a world-class boxer. That part came with dogged determination, grueling hard work, and—mostly—a belief that he was the greatest athlete of all time. But it wasn't his physical prowess that caused Cassius Clay to become what he believed himself to be—it was simply that he refused to stop believing.

During that time in American history, many people couldn't fathom a black man being so presumptuous as to flaunt the anthem, "I'm the greatest!" Many people were enraged when Cassius changed his name to Muhammad Ali. "I don't have to be what you want me to be; I'm free to be what I want!" he proclaimed.

The scrawny kid who refused to believe what other people thought about him won a gold medal in the 1960 Olympics. He battled George Foreman in "The Rumble in the Jungle" in Zaire. He went head to head with Joe Frazier in "The Thrilla in Manila" in the Philippines. He became exactly what he believed he would be; he became the king of the ring.

KING OF THE COMPUTER

In the spring of 1968, the faculty of the Lakeside Prep School recognized that to adequately prepare their students for the future, they had to find a way to introduce them to the world of computers. Back then, computers were too large and costly for the school to buy. A creative solution to their problem was to buy computer time for their students on equipment owned by General Electric.

Fascinated by the world of computers, young Bill Gates stayed in the computer room day and night, writing programs and reading computer literature. He fell behind in all his other classes, turning in homework late or not at all. He skipped classes to spend extra time on the computer.

Without a doubt, God had installed all the equipment in Bill Gates to make him the king of computers. But it was Gates' decision to work out what was inside of him. In 1973, Bill enrolled at Harvard University as a pre-law student. The following year the cover of a magazine touted the "World's First Microcomputer Kit to Rival Commercial Models."

Bill Gates understood what millions of people did not: the home computer market was about to explode and someone would have to develop the software for their use. He was audacious enough to believe he could do it. Bill Gates walked away from a career in law. He walked away from Harvard University. He formed Microsoft, and the rest is history.

Today, he is among the 1 percent of the most influential people in the world. He has affected every nation in the world. And he is the richest man on earth.

DARE TO COMPARE

You're probably wondering how I can dare to compare you to Michael Jordan, Mohammad Ali, or Bill Gates. I don't know their spiritual state, but I can venture to guess yours. The Bible puts it this way:

These men belong to this world, so, quite naturally, they are concerned about worldly affairs and the world pays attention to them. But we are children of God.

(1 John 4:5–6 TLB)

Michael Jordan, Mohammad Ali, and Bill Gates believed they had the right equipment on the inside, and they were willing to work it out. You, who have the God of the universe residing inside of you, constantly put limitations on yourself.

"My skin isn't the right color."

"I don't have the right education."

"There's not enough money in my account."

"I can't afford to follow my dreams."

Here is the difference: Jordan, Ali, and Gates believed what was on the inside mattered; you believe what is on the outside matters. Guess what? They're right; you're wrong!

The key to becoming part of the 1 percent is believing what is inside of you, and being willing to work it out.

What is man that You are mindful of him, and the son of man that You visit him? For You have made him a little lower than the angels, and You have crowned him with glory and honor. You have made him to have dominion over the works of Your hands; You have put all things under his feet. (Psalm 8:4–6)

To Come from God

One day you heard the good news that Jesus had already reconciled you to God, so you went to Him. God filled you with the very best—Himself—then sent you back into the world. In order to come from God, you have to go to God.

Abraham went to God a crippled old man. He came from God a nation of people that shook the world. Moses went to God an insecure, stammering man. He came from God a great deliverer who demonstrated to the world what happens when they mess with God's people. Fishermen and tax collectors went to God full of sin. They came from God filled with such faith and holiness they turned the world upside down.

> In order to come *from* God, you have to go *to* God.

Today, God is expecting you, who have come to Him, to go back to the world with His purpose. He is expecting you to change the world.

> *If my people will humble themselves and pray, and search for me, and turn from their wicked ways, I will hear them from heaven and forgive their sins and heal their land. I will listen, wide awake, to every prayer made in this place.*
> (2 Chronicles 7:14–15 TLB)

FAITH NEEDS AN ENVIRONMENT

"That's all well and good," you might say, "but I don't need to know how to become part of the 1 percent. Right now, I need to know how to get money in my bank account."

That's what I'm telling you! If you get a revelation of who God is and who He is in you, you'll have faith for the rest. But your faith needs an environment in which to operate at its best. You've been running around trying to make your faith work, but you haven't been taking care of your environment.

> *So then faith comes by hearing, and hearing by the word of God.*
> (Romans 10:17)

39

You're not taking care of what goes on around you. You're not taking care of what goes into your heart. You're not taking care of what goes into your ears. You're not taking care of what goes into your eyes. How can you influence the world if you can't even influence your own household?

The Word of God is good seed. Your heart is good ground. So what's the problem? You pray and nothing seems to happen. You don't sense God's presence. There is a drought over your life, and you need the rain of God.

You may be shocked at what I tell you to do: stop trying to make things happen. When God shows up, things will start to happen! When He arrives on the scene, mountains shake. On the day of Pentecost, God showed up and tongues of fire rained down. The apostles didn't make it happen! All they did was obey God. They showed up and they prayed. God did everything else.

CONFESSION:

> Father, it's a big step for me, but I'm asking that You make me part of the 1 percent. I ask that You would reveal what You have put inside of me, and show me how to work it out. I honestly desire to be all that You created me to be. Thank You, Lord. Amen.

FAITH KEY #3—THE ONE PERCENT

In what area of life do you suspect God has called you to be a part of the 1 percent? How can you work what is on the inside of you—out?

If you have no idea how to answer those questions, take time from your schedule to seek God. Ask Him who He created you to be. Ask who He desires to be in you.

The One Percent

I will instruct you (says the Lord) and guide you along the best pathway for your life; I will advise you and watch your progress. (Psalm 32:8 TLB)

Key #4

SEPARATE YOURSELF

Negative People Will Drain You

Everyone owns a little piece of the atmosphere. Yours is whatever you take authority over. It is in that area that you must begin to tear down old influences. You must tear down old behaviors. You must separate yourself from sin.

In order to do that, there is a key to victorious living that many people overlook: you have to separate yourself from negative people.

They will drain your faith. They will drain your energy. They will drain your peace. They will drain your enthusiasm. They will suck the very life out of you. Negative people don't want you to get them out of the rut they're in. They want you to join them in their rut so they don't feel so badly. Someone defined a *rut* as "a grave with both ends kicked out."

Then the children of Israel who had returned from the captivity ate together with all who had separated themselves

Separate Yourself

from the filth of the nations of the land in order to seek the LORD *God of Israel.*   (Ezra 6:21)

RUN FOR YOUR LIFE

Negative people live in maintenance mode. All they want to do is maintain. They don't want to move up. They don't want to move out. They don't want to do anything, except be the center of their own pity party.

The moment you start separating yourself from that attitude, they will start calling you a "dreamer." They don't want you to receive anything new in your life, because they are certain that nothing new will come to them.

A negative attitude is as malignant as cancer. You have to separate yourself from those people. Don't walk—run! Why? Because the atmosphere you permit will determine the product you produce.

Negative people always want to blame someone for their problems. They want to blame their mothers. They want to blame their fathers. They want to blame their bosses. They want to blame their childhoods. They want to blame their education. They'll blame you if you hang around long enough. They may not say it in so many words, but in their hearts, they really blame God.

THEY WILL HOLD BACK YOUR PROMISES

We're so used to living around negativity that we sometimes fail to see it as God sees it. To truly understand God's heart on the matter, just think back to how the Lord brought Israel out of slavery in Egypt with great signs and miracles. He performed mighty miracles to entice Pharaoh to release them.

43

He parted the Red Sea and led them through on dry ground!
Yet when it was time to enter the land God that had promised
to give them, two things happened. First, all but two of the
spies who were sent in to check out the land came back with
negative reports:

> *The land is full of warriors, the people are powerfully built,
> and we saw some of the Anakim there, descendants of the
> ancient race of giants. We felt like grasshoppers before them,
> they were so tall!* (Numbers 13:32–33 TLB)

Second, most of the people believed them.

God didn't say, "Well, bless your hearts, I wish you weren't
so negative, but I love you anyway."
No, He said something along these
lines: "If you boys think you're going
into the Promised Land now, you've
got another big thing coming. Only
Joshua and Caleb gave a positive
report, and only Joshua and Caleb
are going in. All the rest of you will die in the desert." (See
Numbers 14:11–30.)

> If you don't think
> the crowd you hang
> out with matters,
> think again!

The sin of some men speaking a negative report, and of
others believing a negative report, had dire consequences. That
entire generation of Israelites wandered in the desert for forty
years and died without seeing God's promise fulfilled. Caleb
and Joshua did enter the Promised Land and took it from the
giants who had scared everyone else forty years before. (See
Joshua 1:1–3.)

But I want you to think about something: the sin of the
negative crowd around Joshua and Caleb held back their
promise for forty years!

If you don't think the crowd you hang out with matters, you had better think again.

A DEADLY DEAL

Most people are affected by negative people. Millions of Israelites were affected by the negative report of the spies. And God sees that as a slap against Him. How can you be negative if you honestly believe God? What power on earth can stop you if God is with you?

Negative attitudes, like negative friends, can be deadly.

This is not some theoretical concept I learned somewhere. It's scriptural, and it's also a reality I've learned through experience. When I was a young man, my friends smoked marijuana, so I smoked it too. My friends chased women, so I chased them too. My friends blew good opportunities, so I blew mine too. Looking back, I wonder what I expected. I chose to surround myself with people who made negative life decisions, while I hoped to succeed.

But even in the midst of a messed up situation, you can turn things around by changing your atmosphere. Do what I did: I changed friends. I made friends with positive people who made positive choices. It was one of the major missing keys to success in my life. It's equally important in yours.

CONFESSION:

Father, please forgive my negative thoughts, negative attitudes, and negative words. I repent because I now realize that negativity is nothing but slander against You. If I really believe You are with me, how can I be negative? I ask that You help me recognize negative thoughts when they arise and deal with them immediately. I ask that You reveal to me those people in my life who are negative and help me separate myself from them. Amen.

FAITH KEY #4—SEPARATE YOURSELF

First, repent for all the specific ways in which you have been negative. Then ask yourself this question: what negative influences (including friends) have drained the faith and energy from my life?

Make a plan for change, today.

"And as for you, O my flock—my people," the Lord God says, "I will judge you and separate good from bad, sheep from goats."　　　　　　(Ezekiel 34:17 TLB)

Key #5

ATTITUDE IS EVERYTHING

A Bad Attitude Deflates Your Faith

In corporate America, most people who lose their jobs do so, not because they can't do the work, but because of their attitude. Many of them may be able to do the work better than anyone else. But they lose their job because they have a bad attitude about what they're doing.

There is nothing in the world you cannot do—if you set your mind to do it. If you can't do your job, it's because you haven't set your mind to it. If you're really honest, you probably didn't want the job in the first place. You may have wanted the money, but not the job. If you really wanted the job, you'd do your very best instead of complaining about the work.

You cannot live by other people's sloppy standards. You were called to be the best. You've been to God, and you've come into the world to represent Him. You have a whole new set of standards—God's standards. *"I warn you, you yourselves are in danger of punishment for your attitude"* (Job 19:29 TLB).

47

MEASURE YOUR OWN SUCCESS

Life was created by God. The way you respond to your life is the way it will respond to you. You've been given dominion over everything on earth, and the measure you give is the measure it will be given back to you. (See Genesis 1:28 and Mark 4:24.) If you have a negative, sloppy, "I-just-want-my-paycheck attitude," that's the way life will treat you. If you have a winning attitude, you'll end up being a winner.

Most people don't understand that attitude even affects spiritual forces. For instance, faith will not work with a bad attitude. It's a lot like a flat tire; you're not going anywhere until you change it. I don't care if you're the first person to the office each morning and the last to leave. You won't go anywhere until your attitude lines up with God's.

> *Your attitude must be like my own, for I, the Messiah, did not come to be served, but to serve, and to give my life as a ransom for many.* (Matthew 20:28 TLB)

SPIRIT OF EXCELLENCE

Jesus Christ has imparted a spirit of excellence to you. It's standard equipment for a Christian, so it's there even if no one has ever had the pleasure of seeing it. *"Now your attitudes and thoughts must all be constantly changing for the better"* (Ephesians 4:23 TLB).

There is a fighter inside of you.

There is a finisher inside of you.

But you haven't tapped into His help.

Here's what happens. You're afraid of obstacles in your life. When trouble comes your way, you fail. When you fail, you get upset. When you get upset, you get a bad attitude. You look at someone who is succeeding and get jealous. "Why are they succeeding and I'm not? I did the same thing they did. Why did I lose my job? I work harder than anyone else."

A relaxed attitude lengthens a man's life; jealousy rots it away. (Proverbs 14:30 TLB)

God never intended for you to fail. You were created to succeed. Failure is not what He placed inside you.

And the LORD will make you the head and not the tail; you shall be above only, and not be beneath.
(Deuteronomy 28:13)

God desires that you succeed at everything you set your hand to do.

Your attitude can derail His whole plan for your life.

A bad attitude will undermine your success.

It can stop your faith in its tracks.

Your re-created spirit is just waiting for the devil to show up, but your head never got the message. It couldn't hear the battle cry over the roar of your negative attitude.

Attitude is everything.

The world does not give you a mirror that reflects who you are in Christ. In fact, the world will tell you just the opposite. Your job will not show you that reflection. Your family will not remind you each day. You won't find your identity on the Discovery Channel. The highest grossing movie of all time will not show you a picture of who you are. And there is no guarantee that you will discover that truth in church.

There's only one place you will find your true reflection in Christ: in the Word of God.

It is essential that you stay focused on the new you—the re-created person you became when you went to God.

When you change your attitude, you have to build a whole new you. You are a new creature, called and predestined to become the image of Christ.

CONFESSION:

Father, I pray that You open my eyes to see my own attitudes and motives. I ask that You forgive me for not giving my best effort every day and in every way. Help me to have the best attitude and give the best performance on the job, at home with my family, and in everything I do. Help me to have a great attitude about serving You.

FAITH KEY #5—ATTITUDE IS EVERYTHING

List all the bad attitudes you've tolerated in yourself. Then repent of each one and make an uncompromised decision to be the best—even in attitude.

May God who gives patience, steadiness, and encouragement help you to live in complete harmony with each other—each with the attitude of Christ toward the other.

(Romans 15:5 TLB)

Key #6

LOOK AT YOUR REFLECTION

Discover Your True Identity

In the beginning was the Word, and the Word was with God, and the Word was God. He was in the beginning with God. All things were made through Him, and without Him nothing was made that was made. In Him was life, and the life was the light of men. (John 1:1–4)

The Bible makes it clear that Jesus is the Word of God. If you are created in His image, then the Word of God is the mirror that will reflect that image back to you. You will never fulfill your destiny if you do not stay in the Word of God. Putting the Word of God inside of you will cause Christ to be reflected to the world. We are told how to gain wisdom and health in Proverbs 4:20–23:

My son, give attention to my words; incline your ear to my sayings. Do not let them depart from your eyes; keep them in the midst of your heart; for they are life to those who find them, and health to all their flesh. Keep your heart with all diligence, for out of it spring the issues of life.

How can you diligently keep your heart? You keep it by inclining your ear to God's Word. When you read the Word of God so often that it is the first thing to come out of your mouth when trouble strikes, you are not letting it depart from your eyes.

You can't do this by just reading along with your pastor on Sunday morning. You can't get enough in your Sunday school or Bible study. Those things are good, but they aren't good enough. To keep the Word before your eyes, you need to read it every day. You need to hear it to build your faith. Listen to the Word of God on tape. Put Scriptures on your desk, computer screensaver, or mirror. Don't let it depart from your eyes!

> A steady diet of the Word of God is the best antidote for fear.

More than that, blessed are those who hear the word of God and keep it! (Luke 11:28)

A steady diet of the Word of God is the best antidote for fear, or for facing any of the obstacles that confront you. The Word of God will strengthen your spirit man and turn you into a person of great faith.

The Word of God will cut away those things that weigh you down and keep you from running your race to win. It will keep what God put inside of you running smoothly. And it will work what is in you—out.

For the word of God is living and powerful, and sharper than any two-edged sword, piercing even to the division of soul and spirit, and of joints and marrow, and is a discerner of the thoughts and intents of the heart.

(Hebrews 4:12)

The Word of God will do a creative work in you.

It will reach into you and take hold of what it takes to make you part of the 1 percent.

It will let you know you are seated with Jesus in heavenly places.

It will roar with the authority of God when you speak, "Peace!" to the winds and waves that beset you.

It will cause you to win and not to lose.

It will cause you to be the head and not the tail.

It will do what no man on earth can do: it will make you into the person God created you to be.

By faith we understand that the worlds were framed by the word of God, so that the things which are seen were not made of things which are visible. (Hebrews 11:3)

Let God's Word be the final word on your life.

Stay focused on that reflection, and that's what you will become.

CONFESSION:

Father help me see a reflection of myself as You see me. Empower me to keep Your Word before my eyes. Let it guard my heart. Cause Your Word to become alive in me!

53

FAITH KEY #6—LOOK AT YOUR REFLECTION

If staying in the Word of God is like looking in a mirror that reflects Jesus, how much of Jesus is being reflected in you each day? What lifestyle changes can you implement to keep the Word of God before your eyes and in your heart?

So then faith comes by hearing, and hearing by the word of God. (Romans 10:17)

MAKE THE CHANGE

Just Do It!

Change doesn't happen when you think about it. Change doesn't happen when you plan to do it. If that were the case, every smoker would have given up cigarettes by now. Each of us would wear the same size belt we wore in college. But, the truth is, change doesn't happen—until you change.

You can make a list of foods you're going to eat when you change your lifestyle. You can plan your new exercise program. You can pray for successful weight loss. But you won't change who you are until you change what you do.

You may be ready to implement the missing keys to success in life. You may have made a mental note of the people you need to separate yourself from. You may have an idea of a new friend you want to make. You may have been convicted about your bad attitude. And you may have bought a devotional Bible to help you stay in the Word of God.

You know what to do.

But has anything changed?

Of course not! If knowing were all it took, we would all have a Ph.D. in successful living and not struggle with it anymore.

So why hasn't anything changed?

The honest answer is that you're not tired enough of your situation yet. When you are, you'll stop making plans and simply make the change.

> *You will be to me as an offering of perfumed incense when I bring you back from exile, and the nations will see the great change in your hearts.* (Ezekiel 20:41 TLB)

CONFESSION:

> Father, I know that You're waiting for me to make the change. I ask for Your grace to empower me to make every change I need to make in order to walk a victorious life. I repent of planning all my tomorrows and ignoring my today. This day, I choose Your way. Amen.

FAITH KEY #7—MAKE THE CHANGE

Are you tired enough of the situations in your life to actually make a change? If so, implement them. In addition, tell at least one other person to whom you can make yourself accountable.

> *No, a real Jew is anyone whose heart is right with God. For God is not looking for those who cut their bodies in actual*

body circumcision, but he is looking for those with changed hearts and minds. Whoever has that kind of change in his life will get his praise from God, even if not from you.

(Romans 2:29 TLB)

Key #8

LET YOUR FAITH GET VIOLENT

You Will Never Fulfill Your Destiny by Politely Asserting Your Rights

The world will tell you that a key to successful living is being assertive. That sounds good, doesn't it? Assertive is a compromise somewhere between being a wimp and being aggressive. It means you should politely assert your rights. There's only one little problem with this reasoning—the devil doesn't respond to politeness.

When Satan tries to impose himself on you, true faith will get violent.

Don't misunderstand; I'm not suggesting that you get violent with people. You're in a spiritual battle, and faith is a spiritual force.

And from the days of John the Baptist until now the king-dom of heaven suffers violence, and the violent take it by force.   (Matthew 11:12)

"The violent take it by force" isn't very politically correct, is it? But you won't survive standing against the forces of hell trying to be polite. God says *"the violent take it by force,"* and that's exactly how you'll have to win your faith battles.

GIVE FAITH A CHANCE

First Samuel 30 tells the story of David and his mighty men returning from battle to find their wives and children had been taken captive. Scripture doesn't tell us how long the men wept, but it says they cried until there were no more tears. When they stopped crying, they got angry: *"David was greatly distressed, for the people spoke of stoning him, because the soul of all the people was grieved, every man for his sons and his daughters"* (verse 6).

David, the mighty man of God, sat there weeping.

Then he did the unexpected.

Scripture says that *"David strengthened himself in the LORD his God"* (verse 6).

If you give faith the right atmosphere, it will strengthen and encourage you. When things start to go wrong, your faith will stand up and talk to you—if you'll listen.

"Why are you crying, David?" his faith must have said. "Remember when the lion came after you? Didn't God give you the power to kill it with your bare hands? What about the bear? You grabbed him by the chin and killed him. Don't you remember that giant, Goliath, who shouted blasphemies against God's army? You killed him with nothing more than

Faith always gets back everything the devil has stolen.

a slingshot and five smooth stones! Don't just sit there crying! Have you forgotten who you are? Get up and praise God!"

His men wanted to stone him, but David asked God what to do.

So David inquired of the Lord, saying, "Shall I pursue this troop? Shall I overtake them?" And He answered him, "Pursue, for you shall surely overtake them and without fail recover all." (1 Samuel 30:8)

Faith always gets back everything the devil has stolen.

But you have to give faith the atmosphere it needs to operate at its best.

David attacked them from twilight until the evening of the next day. Not a man of them escaped, except four hundred young men who rode on camels and fled. So David recovered all that the Amalekites had carried away, and David rescued his two wives. And nothing of theirs was lacking, either small or great, sons or daughters, spoil or anything which they had taken from them; David recovered all.

(verses 17–19)

David understood that he could sit around weeping forever, or he could request an audience with the Most High. He knew that he could "*enter into His gates with thanksgiving, and into His courts with praise*" (Psalm 100:4).

David was the youngest son, not the eldest.

He was a shepherd boy who went to God.

He came out a King.

60

David was a forefather of Jesus! Of all the people in the history of the world, David became part of the 1 percent.

He marked the path for you to follow.

Strengthen yourself in the Lord and let your faith get violent.

CONFESSION:

> Father, I ask that You give me the grace for me to change the atmosphere around me so that my faith can flourish. Help me to encourage myself in You. I ask that what You put on the inside of me would work its way out to change the world. I repent of false humility. I am a warrior with violent faith like David. Like him, I will give You all the glory. Amen.

FAITH KEY #8—
LET YOUR FAITH GET VIOLENT

Think back to all the ways God has helped you in the past. Lift weary hands to the Lord and thank Him. Enter his gates with thanksgiving and His courts with praise. Strengthen yourself in the Lord. Seek God's strategy for returning to you everything the devil has stolen. Let your faith get violent. Pursue, attack, and recover all!

> *Think of the mighty deeds he did for us, his chosen ones— descendants of God's servant Abraham, and of Jacob. Remember how he destroyed our enemies. He is the Lord our God. His goodness is seen everywhere throughout the land. Though a thousand generations pass he never forgets his promise.* (Psalm 105:5–8 TLB)

Key #9

REFUSE TO BE LIMITED BY YOUR LIMITATIONS

Step out of Your Box

On a visit to Mexico, my wife, Connie, and I saw both extravagant prosperity and abject poverty. We saw multimillion-dollar mansions perched atop mountains. Only minutes away, we saw families huddled in houses with no roofs or doors. "These people are going to have an opportunity to move into a nice condominium or a mansion in the hills," I told Connie. "I believe there will be a major transfer of wealth in the world's system, but God isn't just going to take from the rich and give to the poor. I think the transfer of wealth will be based on people's knowledge of the Word of God, and their refusal to be limited by their limitations."

I'm convinced that God is trying to get His people to prepare for what's ahead.

God wants us to be the best on earth. After all, we are a reflection of Him. He is not average and He is not a part of the status quo. If you have really died to yourself and now are alive in Him, then your life should reflect His.

If you're satisfied with your life, chances are you have fallen short of God's best. I want to challenge you to live beyond your limitations.

We're conditioned to living in a box with walls made of our own expectations and belief systems. Most of them were formed by listening to the world and our own negative self talk. If that weren't bad enough, we've tried to squeeze God into our box of beliefs. I've got news for you: God will not fit in anyone's box, and He's demanding that those who follow Him climb out of theirs.

> If you have died to self and live in Him, your life should reflect His.

God wants to strip you of your boundaries and replace them with His own. As Jesus stretched forth His hand toward Lazarus' tomb and commanded, *"Come forth!"* (John 11:43), I believe that today the Lord is stretching out His hand to those of us entombed in a box of our own limitations. He's commanding, *"Come forth!"*

Those who have ears to hear, and the courage to obey, will move into a life of abundance over and above anything they could imagine. Because, the truth is, we can't imagine what God has planned for us. It is beyond our ability to comprehend. That's why moving out of our box is such a step of faith—we don't know where He'll lead us! But we know assuredly that He will lead us into situations that we are utterly unable to handle in our own strength.

That, of course, is the whole point.

That's exactly where He wants us.

If our lives are limited to what we can do, God is in our box.

> *Now when He had said these things, He cried with a loud voice, "Lazarus, come forth!" And he who had died came out bound hand and foot with graveclothes, and his face was wrapped with a cloth. Jesus said to them, "Loose him, and let him go."* (John 11:43–44)

GOD IN RESIDENCE

When you became born again, God moved in. That's what 1 Corinthians 3:16 means when it says, *"Do you not know that you are the temple of God and that the Spirit of God dwells in you?"*

According to the Bible, your body is the temple of God. The blood of Jesus bought you back from slavery to sin, and God has moved in. He is repossessing His property! Your body, now God's temple, is no longer your own, and God is no slum lord! As the new and rightful owner, He has begun renovations. He is filling you with Himself.

There's only one problem: the current state of your heart is too small, and it has to be enlarged. God has a new architectural plan that includes knocking out some walls and doing major expansions. After all, God is used to living in the best. But these renovations aren't just for His sake; they're for ours as well.

But, in our hearts, we have already limited God. How have you limited God? You've limited Him by believing that the wage you make now is the best you'll ever do. You've limited Him by believing that because you're not in full-time ministry, you can't possibly change the world. You've limited Him by believing that you'll never be part of the 1 percent. You've limited Him by believing that all you can accomplish in life are those things you can do in your own strength. You've limited Him by believing that you're limited by your circumstances, your socioeconomic situation, your gender, or your race. You've limited Him by believing that there's no way for you to further your education. You've limited Him by believing that because your mother had diabetes, you'll have it too. You've limited Him by believing that your whole family is genetically conditioned to be overweight, and that's all you can expect. You've limited Him by turning your back on your deepest dreams.

GOD PROVIDES THE TRAINING

I was working in a cubicle at Sun Oil Company when God put it on my heart to start my own computer consulting company. After much prayer, I went to my boss and shared my dream in the hope that he might offer advice, encouragement, and maybe even hire the services of my new company.

Instead, he got a little upset and told me, "You're not going to make it! You can't even talk! How are you going to make it in business?" He continued to try to discourage me, but he couldn't.

I went back to my desk and there came a knock on my cubicle. It was the gentleman who owned the company that did most of the consulting work at Sun. He was doing what God was calling me to do with my new business. This man said that my manager sent him to tell me how rough and difficult the consulting business could be.

He began to warn me of all the things he had to go through, all the people he had to deal with, and all the places he had to go. As he was talking, I realized that he was telling me how to run his business. And since I had no knowledge of how to run his business, I started taking notes. God had sent somebody to show me how to run the business that He was calling me to start.

At the end, this man went away thinking that he had successfully discouraged me by giving me so much information that I wouldn't want to do it. But when he left, I was rejoicing because I now had an entire business plan mapped out based on all the things he said. It was a proven plan because it came from his business. Therefore, by the time I went to the bank, my plan wasn't based on what I wanted; it was based on what had already been done. It was based on a proven model of success.

Never let the world dissuade you in following something that God has called you to do. He gave you those dreams!

Ask God to give you enough determination, persistence, and willpower to break out of your box and remove every limitation from your life.

You've had your limit of limitations.

CONFESSION:

> Father, forgive me for living in the confines of my own limitations. Forgive me for trying to fit You in my box of doubt and unbelief. Help me stop looking at my limitations and look to You—the author and finisher of my faith!

FAITH KEY #9—
REFUSE TO BE LIMITED BY YOUR LIMITATIONS

Make a list of all the hopes and dreams that you let go over the years. Ask God to resurrect them. Now, prophetically command them, *"Come forth!"*

Refuse to Be Limited by Your Limitations

Make another list of all the limitations you've lived with. Repent for doubting God's power over each limitation on your list.

Make a third list of your new goals. Find Scripture that supports your belief that God will help you live beyond your limitations. Put them in your Bible, tape them to your mirror, post them on your refrigerator, and keep them before your eyes.

Pray over them.

Live them.

"I can do all things through Christ who strengthens me."
(Philippians 4:13)

Key #10

DO A NEW THING!

If You Want Something You Have Never Had, You Must Do Something You Have Never Done

This key to victorious living is so important that it is a motto to live by: if you want something you have never had, you must do something you've never done.

It doesn't matter what you want, whether it is a new career, a college education, a retirement account, money in the bank, or something as crucial as a successful professional or private life. But it won't happen until you do something you've never done. You simply can't keep doing whatever it is that you've been doing if you don't want to keep experiencing the status quo.

There's an old saying that's tried and true: the definition of insanity is doing the same thing over and over and expecting different results. Yet most of us get trapped on that treadmill of our minds that causes us to keep taking the same steps, but going nowhere.

RENOVATION IN PROGRESS

You can stop the treadmill by awaking every morning with this thought: *God is doing a new thing in me today.* The Holy Spirit is at work inside of you, doing major renovations. If you don't know that, you won't cooperate with Him by beginning the process of working out what He's working in.

And I am sure that God who began the good work within you will keep right on helping you grow in his grace until his task within you is finally finished on that day when Jesus Christ returns. (Philippians 1:6 TLB)

Most people can't see what God is doing in you. Only the people that are close to you may sense that something is changing. But the truth is, you can't see what God is doing inside of you except through the eyes of faith.

God is constantly measuring you. He's constantly chipping away at those old things that you don't need in your new life. He's constantly moving things around to restore you back to your original purpose.

Just as God spoke all of creation into existence, the Bible says that you were created by the Word of God. (See Genesis 1:26.) So how is He recreating you? By the Word of God! The Word becomes His hammer. The Word becomes His nails. The Word becomes a board. The Word becomes a foundation.

<u>Everything you need comes from the Word of God.</u>

Do you need more love in your life? Do you need more joy? Do you need more peace? All of these things and more come from the Word of God.

God is enlarging your thinking. Remember when you used to think, *I just can't do that!* There was a time when you thought

69

you couldn't ride a bicycle. There was a time when you thought you couldn't drive a car. But now you can do those things. God is continually stretching your thinking to remove limitations.

But you have a part in this process! Paul said that you need to work out what God is working in!

> *Therefore, my beloved, as you have always obeyed, not as in my presence only, but now much more in my absence, work out your own salvation with fear and trembling.*
>
> (Philippians 2:12)

If you start working out what God is working in, then things will change in your life, in your household, in your family, and in your business. Things all around you will start working. Too often, instead of believing God and stepping out in faith, believers simply cry, "Lord, just do it for me!"

> God is continually stretching your thinking to remove limitations.

He is doing it! He's is giving you everything you need for success!

We have too many lazy Christians who want to sit in their recliners and "pop in a tape." They don't want to work out what God has worked in them. They don't want to build up their spiritual muscles. They want someone else to do it for them.

Here is a news flash for you: no one can do it for you!

Sure, other people can pray and intercede on your behalf. Other people can spoon-feed the Word of God to you. But they can't make your spiritual muscles go to work. They can't release your faith. Nobody can do that but you!

70

Let me tell you how to work out what God has worked in you. Get in the Word of God. Feed on the Word of God. Meditate on the Word of God. Talk about the Word of God. Sing about the Word of God. Share the Word of God. Start to flex those spiritual muscles. Then think of something you could not have done before—and do it by faith.

This Book of the Law shall not depart from your mouth, but you shall meditate in it day and night, that you may observe to do according to all that is written in it. For then you will make your way prosperous, and then you will have good success. (Joshua 1:8)

MY LIMITATION

I was born with a stutter that worsened over the years. I could think what I wanted to say, but when I tried to speak, the words simply wouldn't come. I was embarrassed and humiliated. By the time I reached high school, I would take an "F" rather than give an oral presentation. I withdrew and spent most of my time alone.

The one exception to that was football. You didn't have to talk in football—just think and act. Out on the field, it didn't matter that I was born with a speech impediment. It didn't matter that kids made fun of me, or that class presentations were their own brand of terror. It didn't matter that my stutter kept me from being captain of the team. It didn't matter that I could never be quarterback because I couldn't call the plays. The only thing that mattered to me was the ball and my team.

There is one particular game that I'll never forget. I can still see the sunlight reflecting off the shining brass instruments and smooth, hardened helmets. Cheerleaders jumped and flipped as the crowd roared its approval. The drum line beat mimicked my racing heart. It was one of the most important games of my high school football career.

CALLING THE PLAY

Every nerve was alive as we fought our way toward victory. We took the lead by a close margin in the second quarter. I ran off the field and high-fived my teammates before grabbing a towel and a long drink of water. The ball changed hands and the excitement was palpable as our team headed for the huddle.

The coached bellowed, "McLean! You're up!"

The coach gave me the play, and I ran into the huddle.

"What's the play?" the quarterback asked.

"C..c..c..coach s..s..s..s..s…."

"Lamont! What did he say?"

"H..h..h..he…s..s..s…."

Every face in the huddle implored me. The clock was ticking. I tried again.

"D..d..d..d..do t..t..t..the…."

"Forget it, we're out of time," the quarterback snapped. "I'll call the play."

The moment we broke the huddle and followed the quarterback's play, coach realized what had happened. As we lost the ball and lost the game, I heard him scream my name from the sidelines.

"McLean!"

I can still taste that bitter disappointment.

But do you know what that game and other situations like it taught me? The same thing I'm trying to teach you: if you want to have something you've never had, you have to do something you've never done.

ROCKING THE BOX

That football game summed up my life. Everything I attempted to do ran right up against the limitation of that stutter. My speech impediment defined my life; it defined what I could do, and what I would never do. When I was born again, God was safely tucked away in a box.

> If you want to have something you've never had, you have to do something you've never done.

At least that's what I thought until the day I ran across a Scripture in Isaiah that changed my life forever:

> *The mind of the rash will have good judgment, and the tongue of the stammerers will speak readily and distinctly.*
> (Isaiah 32:4 RSV)

This sounded to me like God was promising to take me beyond my limitations.

I began to meditate on that verse and confess it. I prayed that God would release my tongue from stammering. Nothing changed outwardly. I stuttered and stammered every time I spoke. But God had moved in. He was doing major renovations inside of me. The more I meditated on that promise, the more I rocked against the box.

I meditated on that Scripture so much that I believed the certainty of God's Word would change the uncertainty of my circumstances.

In 1983, my faith was put to the test.

"Lamont," my pastor said, "I want you to teach Wednesday night Bible study."

My mind reeled and my heart pounded. I could just imagine my pastor standing on the sidelines like my coach, screaming, "McLean!"

Fear and doubt screamed so loud I had to turn my thoughts to God's Word.

I tell you the truth, if anyone says to this mountain, "Go, throw yourself into the sea," and does not doubt in his heart but believes it will happen, it will be done for him. Therefore I tell you, whatever you ask for in prayer, believe that you have received it, and it will be yours. (Mark 11:23–24 NIV)

I knew at that moment that if I ever wanted to live outside the box of my limitations, I would have to lay my doubt, unbelief, fear, and humiliation on the altar before God. Stumbling over my words as I spoke, I agreed to teach the Bible study. Then I studied and prepared the lesson.

God is not looking for ability;

He is looking for availability.

PANIC ATTACK

When the day arrived, I drove across town and broke out in a cold sweat. My palms dripped with perspiration as I gripped the steering wheel. My heart pounded and my lungs tightened. Gasping for air, I pulled the car off the road in the midst of a full-blown panic attack.

It's a fearful thing to break out of your limitations and open the door to your future. I knew that if I didn't walk up to that podium and open my mouth to speak—regardless of the outcome—I would never fulfill my destiny.

That night, I did something I had never done before. I walked up the steps to that podium and spoke—clearly and distinctly—to the congregation. The moment I opened my mouth, the limitations I'd lived with all my life disappeared. I was free to live my life.

That doesn't mean that I never struggled with that speech impediment again. It simply means that the next time I spoke to a group of people, I had to face down my fear again. Again and again, until eventually, I didn't give it a second thought.

I allowed the truth of God's Word on the inside to change my circumstances on the outside.

God had gone to work inside of me and called me back to my original purpose.

He's doing the same thing for you.

"Do not be afraid; only believe" (Mark 5:36).

CONFESSION:

Father, help me do a new thing by faith. Forgive me for being a treadmill Christian—moving but going nowhere. Forgive me for doing the same thing over and over while expecting different results. I ask that You guide me, step by step, as I do things I've never done before. Strengthen my spirit man to become new in You. Amen.

FAITH KEY #10—DO A NEW THING!

What do you want that you've never had? What new thing

will you have to do to get it? Meditate on the Word of God. Meditate on God's ability to do it in you.

Just do it!

Therefore I say to you, whatever things you ask when you pray, believe that you receive them, and you will have them. (Mark 11:24)

Key #11

TRAIN YOURSELF

What You Train Yourself to Do Daily Is What You Will Become

No one does anything great in life unless they train for it. Michael Jordan had to train himself to be in the 1 percent of basketball players. Mohammad Ali had to train himself to be the champ. Bill Gates had to train himself to become the best at computer programming. What most people don't understand is that the same is true when it comes to achieving personal and professional success.

"That may be true," you might say, "but right now, I'm not in training."

You're always in training for something. You may be in training to be the most carnal Christian who ever lived. You may be in training to be the laziest couch potato in creation. Whatever you train yourself to do daily is what you'll become. If you're ready to work out what God has put in you, you must go into training.

There are many parallels between living in the natural and living in the supernatural. One of them is your training regimen. In the natural, you may have a picture on your refrigerator of the body you want. In order to reach your goal, you develop a plan to eat right and exercise—daily. If you reward yourself by laying on the sofa and munching on potato chips, chances are you'll never reach your goal.

The same is true of your supernatural training regime. The devil will do everything in his power to get you to be a couch-potato Christian. Whichever way you choose to go—you will become what you do daily.

THE MEANING OF MEDITATION

How do you train yourself spiritually? You do it by meditating on the Word of God. The New Age movement has given meditation a bad rap, but meditating on the Word was around long before gurus chanting a mantra, and is perfectly scriptural. The Hebrew word for *meditate* has many meanings. One of them is "mental exercise and planning." The more you meditate on the Word of God and let it sink deep within you, the more your mind will be transformed to think along those lines.

Interestingly enough, there are several other distinct Hebrew definitions for the word *meditate*. One definition is "to moan" and refers to the moaning of a dove. A dove's moan is similar to a coo and runs like a small motor—continually. If you hold a dove, you will hear its moan.

In Scripture, the dove always represents the Holy Spirit. When you hear the Word of God, the Holy Spirit within you will start to moan. When you hear a preacher preach the heart of God, that little motor on the inside of you will start to hum.

When you meditate on the Word of God, you allow the Holy Spirit to impart fresh revelation that goes to work on your inner man and renews your mind.

The second Hebrew meaning of *mediation* is "to mutter." If you keep meditating, eventually you will begin to mutter.

"I don't see why I can't be the best."

"God is in me, so I can be the best."

That's when you start talking to God. You start having conversations about the Word that you've been meditating on. You start to mature in Christ.

Finally, a third meaning for *meditate* in Hebrew is "to speak." Eventually you'll mutter so long in meditation that God will tell you to stop talking to yourself. He'll say, "Let me show you what I have for you." That's when you start speaking what God has shown you. You aren't saying it just to say it. It's no formula. Now you say it because you know beyond a shadow of doubt that you will have what you say. The Word has created a new level of faith and authority in you. You declare, "I believe! And I receive it now in Jesus' name!"

MEDITATION EMPOWERS YOUR FAITH

I want you to understand this principle in very practical terms. The best example of this happened when I went deep-sea fishing in Mexico. I'd never been on a fishing trip like that one. For the first time, I understood the disciples saying, *"We have toiled all night and caught nothing"* (Luke 5:5). I learned what it feels like to have the waves toss you about until you cry, *"Teacher, do You not care that we are perishing?"* (Mark 4:38).

I didn't know a thing about deep-sea fishing, and at least half the men on the boat couldn't speak a word of English.

The captain couldn't speak English. The first mate couldn't speak English. I couldn't speak Spanish. And we were out in the Pacific Ocean for two miserable days. That boat bucked until every man on it was begging to see land. But all we saw were more waves coming at us.

The food got wet and ruined, but that wouldn't have mattered anyway because most of the men were throwing up over the side of the boat. Here is the sad truth: I never saw a fish. I was never so glad to get off a boat in my life.

On the third day, Pastor Goudeaux arrived and caught fish. I went horseback riding and meditated on the Word of God all day long. The next day Pastor talked us into climbing into that boat again and putting out to sea. None of those men knew that I'd been meditating on being the best. I hadn't caught a thing the last time I went out, but inside I knew I was the best. The next thing I knew, there was a fish on my line giving me the fight of my life. It felt like my shoulder would come out of its socket.

"Guide the line!" Pastor shouted, beating me on the shoulder.

"Stop beating me! The fish is bad enough!"

He pounded me so hard he knocked off my watch. "Forget the watch! Guide the line!"

Finally, I got the fish in the boat. I'll tell you the honest truth: I'd been moaning and meditating about being the best until that fish hit my line. That first fish was a trophy, and I wanted another. I was speaking now; I called in another fish.

The next thing I knew, I was reeling in another big fish.

Pastor Goudeaux started groaning. "Oh, man! Shoot!" I thought I'd done something wrong. "You caught a Rooster

Fish!" he said. "I've never caught one. In fact, I've never even seen anyone catch one!"

Listen, I was calling those things that are not as though they were. I'd meditated enough. I didn't know anything about fishing, but I was the man. I said, "All three of those rods are going to catch fish at the same time."

Pastor Goudeaux gave me a long look and said, "I'm not going to argue with your faith, brother."

Suddenly, three fish hit all three of our lines at the exact same time. You've never seen anything like the scrambling on that boat. They reeled theirs in, and the biggest tuna of the day was on my line. I brought that bad boy in.

A SPIRITUAL PRINCIPLE

I shared that story with you so that you'll understand that this isn't magic, and it isn't rocket science. Meditation on the Word of God sets spiritual principles in place. It will work in you the same as it worked in me. Some may call that fishing experience luck, but I know better. Luck didn't make everything I said come to pass.

> The things you meditate on daily are what you'll become.

I want you to understand that the things you meditate on daily are what you'll become. Meditation is the incubator for your faith, and I can assure you that you will never prosper without it.

And since we have the same spirit of faith, according to what is written, "I believed and therefore I spoke," we also believe and therefore speak. (2 Corinthians 4:13)

REAL FAITH

There are a lot of misconceptions about faith. Real faith isn't "Name It and Claim It." Nor is it "Blab It and Grab It." The Scripture says that we believe and then we speak. If you think you are going to get whatever you say, you are missing the point of this Scripture. You do not receive things simply by speaking.

Too many people want to take a shortcut to faith. They hear what the preacher said and run around saying it without taking the time to meditate on the Word of God until you believe it so much you have to speak it.

The Bible says that you must first believe. It also says that we are to have the same spirit of faith. A spirit has to be developed. This isn't something you can copy and paste and make work. You must believe—have faith—for this principle to work. If you don't have anything on the inside of you, you can name, claim, blab, and grab all you want, but you'll see no results.

The only way your spirit can grow in faith is through meditation on God's Word. The Bible says that people perish for a lack of knowledge. (See Hosea 4:6.) In other words—ignorance kills. In order to understand the Holy Spirit, you must understand the language the Holy Spirit speaks.

The Holy Spirit speaks faith.

CONFESSION:

Father, teach me to meditate on Your Word. Teach me to train myself to become all that You created me to be.

FAITH KEY #11—TRAIN YOURSELF

Take a good hard look at what you do every day. What are you training yourself to become? What do you meditate on day and night? Is it the Word of God?

Decide where you'd like to be spiritually in the next week, month, and year.

Start training today.

When the Son of man comes, will he find faith on earth?
(Luke 18:8 RSV)

Key #12

GET KNOWLEDGE

$\left(\begin{array}{c}\text{The Difference between Your Present Situation}\\\text{and Your Dreams Is Information}\end{array}\right)$

T his contains a crucial truth. <u>The difference between where you are right now and God's plan for your future is information</u>. According to the Word of God, something specific is destroying lives. God isn't talking about Satan. He isn't talking about all the demons in hell. He isn't talking about your boss, your in-laws, or your ex-wife. God said, *"My people are destroyed for lack of knowledge"* (Hosea 4:6).

In other words, if you are not experiencing personal and professional success, there are only two reasons: either (1) you don't have the information you need, or (2) you have the knowledge, but you are ignoring it. Ignoring wisdom is called ignorance.

What you don't know gives place to the devil. What you do know, but you ignore, also gives place to the devil. For instance, if you have knowledge of true salvation, the devil won't bother you in that area. Why should he waste his time? He'll move on to areas of your life where you don't have, or are ignoring, the information you need.

While you may know that your eternal salvation is settled, you may not know that by Jesus' stripes you are healed. You may not know that you must receive healing by faith—just as you received your salvation. Or you simply may not know how faith works, so the devil will attack in that area of your life.

Perhaps you know that Jesus paid the price for your healing, but you don't know that God desires to prosper you. You may have taken a vow of poverty because you believed that poverty makes you holy. The devil will attack you in that area because your lack of knowledge of the Word of God has given him place. The more you know and understand the Word of God, the more you can shut the devil down.

> What you don't know gives place to the devil.

Too often we want to receive Jesus, but we don't want Him throughout the whole house. We want Him to come in through a window and dwell within a part of our lives—maybe we keep Him in the foyer. We rest in the fact that heaven is our eternal home, but we don't want the Lord Jesus to check out the bedroom or the kitchen.

The same is true in our bodies. Jesus has come in to save us, but we may not know that He's interested in every part of our lives. Whatever part of your life that Jesus does not occupy, the devil does. He's in your living room. He's in your rec room. He's in your bedroom. He's in your bathroom.

Think about the words being spewed out in those places. Think about who is yelling. What's going on in the kid's room?

If what you see is not the precious peace of God, Jesus is not in that place.

Marriages are being destroyed because we don't understand covenant. God's people are broke and in debt because we don't understand the purpose of money. Many people get sick and die because they don't know that God has given them divine health.

Ignorance gives the devil place.

That's why church should be, first and foremost, a place to receive the life-changing information contained in the Word of God. It's wonderful to whoop and holler and shout. There is a time and place for that. But first you should get the information that will move you on to fulfill your dreams. Otherwise, you'll whoop and holler while being stuck in a stagnant situation.

INFORMATION IS POWER

Information is so vitally important, yet the world understands this better than the church. And that's why so many within the church are getting whipped and beaten in life. The world knows and understands that information is power. That's why the world tries to hold back information. They only want to give you enough to get you off their backs.

I look at graduating students who say, "We're going to take the world." I think, *No, you're not going to take anything, because they only give you enough information to keep you from being a drain on society.*

While there's nothing wrong with higher education, I suggest you consider a higher source. God will educate you about your purpose in life. God will give you the information you need to fulfill your dreams.

If you really want to learn how to live your life successfully, follow the advice found in Proverbs 4:

> *He taught me also, and said unto me, Let thine heart retain my words: keep my commands, and live.*
>
> (Proverbs 4:4 KJV)

If you keep God's commandments, you'll live. There is life in the Word of God. <u>When you get the Word of God, you're not just getting information—you're getting wisdom. Wisdom will bring understanding.</u>

> *Get wisdom, get understanding: forget it not; neither decline from the words of my mouth.* (verse 5 KJV)

THE PRINCIPLE THING

According to the Bible, there is one principle thing that will cause you to live in victory. That thing is wisdom. God's wisdom teaches you how to apply knowledge and get the best results. It takes you past knowledge and leads you into God's purpose.

> God's wisdom teaches you how to apply knowledge and get the best results.

> *Get wisdom! Get understanding! Do not forget, nor turn away from the words of my mouth. Do not forsake her, and she will preserve you; love her, and she will keep you. Wisdom is the principal thing; therefore get wisdom. And in all your getting, get understanding. Exalt her, and she will promote you; she will bring you honor, when you embrace her. She will place on your head an ornament of grace; a crown of glory she will deliver to you.* (verses 5–9 KJV)

Wisdom brings promotion, respect, honor, grace, and glory. Get wisdom and you will be respected. Get wisdom and you will be promoted. Get wisdom and you will be honored. Everyone on your job may have the same information you have, but everyone doesn't have the wisdom to put it into practice.

So how do you get the wisdom, knowledge, and understanding to defeat the devil? Jesus gave the answer when He was tempted by the devil:

Then Jesus was led up by the Spirit into the wilderness to be tempted by the devil. And he fasted forty days and forty nights, and afterward he was hungry. And the tempter came and said to him, "If you are the Son of God, command these stones to become loaves of bread." But he answered, "It is written, 'Man shall not live by bread alone, but by every word that proceeds from the mouth of God.'"

(Matthew 4:1–4 RSV)

If you're going to live a victorious life, you cannot live by bread alone; you have to live on every word that proceeds from the mouth of God.

The Word of God has everything you need to know.

CONFESSION:

Father, help me get knowledge. Help me gain the information and the wisdom that I need to live victoriously all the days of my life. I choose now to live on Your Word.

FAITH KEY #12—GET KNOWLEDGE

Take a hard look at your life. Look at the difference between where you are now and where you'll need to be to fulfill your dreams. Ask God for the knowledge to get from here to there. Seek the Word of God daily for the wisdom to follow your dream.

> *"Give me now wisdom and knowledge to go out and come in before this people, for who can rule this thy people, that is so great?" God answered Solomon, "Because this was in your heart, and you have not asked possessions, wealth, honor, or the life of those who hate you, and have not even asked long life, but have asked wisdom and knowledge for yourself that you may rule my people over whom I have made you king, wisdom and knowledge are granted to you. I will also give you riches, possessions, and honor, such as none of the kings had who were before you, and none after you shall have the like."* (2 Chronicles 1:10–12 RSV)

Key #13

FINISH YOUR RACE

You Are Judged by What You Finish— Not by What You Start

God is the Alpha and Omega, the Beginning and the End—His is the first word and the last word. The Bible says that Jesus, the Messiah, is *"the author and finisher of our faith."* That means He always finishes what He starts. When Jesus was led into the wilderness, He finished that work. He finished the work on the cross, bringing redemption to all mankind. Whatever He started, He finished.

> *Therefore we also, since we are surrounded by so great a cloud of witnesses, let us lay aside every weight, and the sin which so easily ensnares us, and let us run with endurance the race that is set before us, looking unto Jesus, the author and finisher of our faith, who for the joy that was set before Him endured the cross, despising the shame, and has sat down at the right hand of the throne of God.*
>
> (Hebrews 12:1–2)

You are created in the likeness and image of God, and that means you were created to finish your assignments too. In Hebrews 12 we are told, *"Looking unto Jesus, the author and finisher of our faith"* (verse 2). Jesus is a finisher, and His great desire is to finish your faith.

"How can I finish what I don't know to do?" you may ask.

First of all you need to understand this: you have an assignment.

Everything God created has an assignment. For instance, in Genesis, God told man to have dominion over the earth. (See Genesis 1:26, 28.) Part of your assignment is to have dominion over your world, which means you've been given an assignment to live successfully—not in failure. That is part of the general assignment given by God to mankind.

But you also have a specific assignment and purpose for your life. It was coded in your genetic makeup when you were born. Most people spend their whole lives trying to figure out what life is about. They wonder, *Where am I going? What am I supposed to do? Who is God?*

A Major Key: Finding Your Purpose

Since your assignment comes from God, no man can tell you what it is. You have to get that information from the throne room of heaven. It is crucial that you ask God, and wait on Him for the answer. This is one of the major missing keys to personal and professional success.

Let's say you enlisted in the Marines, and two weeks later you hadn't gotten your orders giving you your assignment. You were so anxious to get started that you chose a boot camp and showed up. During roll call, your name wasn't on the roster.

Everyone else stood in formation, but you watched from the sidelines. When the other troops did pushups, you watched from a distance and did them too. When they ran five miles, you tagged along behind, trying to keep them in sight. That night everyone else had an assigned bunk but you.

That sounds ridiculous doesn't it? Yet it is exactly what many Christians are doing. They don't take time to get their assignment, so they follow someone else and try to run some-one else's race! Just imagine: God has an army, but most enlisted men and women never wait for their orders. They arrive at a boot camp (church) of their choosing and can't understand why they never seem to find their place. Not knowing what else to do, they get busy "working" for God—a lot like doing pushups on the sidelines and running behind the crowd always trying to keep up.

> Ask God what He has called you to do, and wait for His answer.

They spend their lives doing pushups, running, and exhausting themselves in good works, never understanding why their lives are powerless. It's because they never got their orders! Some of them were assigned to the war room of the Pentagon! Why aren't they serving where they were called? Because they never imagined what God had called them to do. Neither can you imagine your call.

Presumption is not faith. Presumption is a dangerous and deadly sin.

Do not presume to know what God has called you to do! Ask Him! And wait on Him for an answer! Stay sensitive to the Spirit of God, keeping a listening ear for His voice. Be quick to obey and seek His will all the days of your life.

He'll see to it that you fulfill your assignments. He'll finish your faith.

QUITTING IS A LIFESTYLE

Quitting will take you over. All you have to do is quit once and you will develop a lifestyle of quitting.

When I was in high school, I was a letterman in three sports. But I used to look up and see my friends in the stands with all the pretty girls. I began to get mad that they were having all the fun while I was doing all this work.

So, my sophomore year, I played football but decided not to go out for wrestling. The new wrestling coach came to me and personally asked me to go out for the team. Impressed that he would ask me, I went out for the team. But my heart wasn't in it. Wrestling practice is rough. You've got to want it to go through with all that. Finally, I sat on a bench and announced, "I'm done. I'm quitting."

The rest of my sophomore year was spent with my friends in the stands. I decided not to play baseball either. When the next year rolled around, I didn't play football. I was now fully invested in quitting.

Soon I realized that whenever I did something that I didn't like for any reason, I would quit. That bothered me. So, my senior year, I went out for football just to prove that I could beat this quitting. I stayed with it, but all the time I wanted to quit. It was like torture. In the spring I went out for baseball but ended up quitting.

I went on to college with a lot of people from my school. Some of the other players were urging me to go out for football. But this fear of quitting made me not try even though I wanted to do it. Fear now had me because quitting was a part of me. When baseball season arrived, once again my friends were encouraging me to try out. I kept resisting, fearing that I would quit. But they stayed on me. My pride won out so I went out for baseball. In the end, all my friends got cut and I made the team. They were all disappointed and mad and I felt bad because I was on the team and didn't really want to be. I made it through two games and quit.

After my freshman year, I decided I didn't want to go back to college, so I quit.

Next, I signed up for the military, hoping this would help me conquer this lifestyle of quitting. After all, you can't quit the military. But, after a while I didn't like it and I wanted to quit. Of course, my commanding officers told me, "You can't quit the military. Nobody quits the military." But I did it. Somehow, I got out of the military with an honorable discharge. Nobody knows how I did it, but I did it.

I had quit just about everything that I had ever started. It had become my lifestyle. I was a quitter. I got married and within six months I was ready to quit my marriage.

Finally, a close friend said, "Why don't you come to church with me?" To make a long story short, I went to church where I got saved, and the Word of God began to change me from the inside out.

I learned to stop condemning myself for my past. I learned to get past the fear I had of starting things. I learned that it's not how you start something; it's how you finish. If you judge yourself to be a quitter, you will never try. You won't finish anything; you will always be quitting. I learned that there was a spirit associated with this thing and I needed to be delivered from it. I asked God to fill me with His Spirit and His Word that would replace this quitting. I needed Him to renew my mind. When that happened, quitting was no longer in me. I began to let Him help me finish. People began to look at me differently because I was now a finisher instead of a quitter. It's important to understand that when Jesus comes into your life there is no quit in you, because greater is He that lives inside of you.

RUNNING THE RACE

That same Scripture in Hebrews 12 says,

Let us run with endurance the race that is set before us, looking unto Jesus, the author and finisher of our faith.

(verses 1–2)

The first thing we need to realize is that we can't run our race without looking to Jesus. The second thing is that we have a race to run. This is Paul's analogy of your life in Christ Jesus. It's a race, and everyone has a lane. The lane you run in is your assignment. If you get in someone else's lane, you're disqualified. That's why, if you spend your life imitating someone else, you

> The race is about faith in God. It's not important how fast you run it.

will not hear the words, *"Well done, good and faithful servant"* (Matthew 25:21, 23).

You may see a great Christian whom you admire. You think, *I want to be like him or her. I'm going to do what he or she is doing.* But you are so busy trying to get in that person's lane, and running his or her race, you don't even realize you've been disqualified. You cut yourself off from the blessings of God because you moved away from God's plan for your life.

95

The only race you will be judged on is your race.

You get no points for starting well.

You are only judged by what you finish.

That's why it is so important that you keep your eyes on Jesus—*"the author and finisher of your faith."* As soon as you get your eyes off Him, you'll wander outside your lane.

THE RACE IS NOT TO THE SWIFT

It's easy to get discouraged in the race of life. The way it happens is that you take your eyes off Jesus and watch the fast runners that pass you, leaving you in their dust. You're trudging along far behind the pack, certain that this couldn't possibly be the race God called you to run. The devil wars against your mind, telling you that you're a loser and that you've failed God.

In those times, it's vital that you know that it's not about how fast you are. Solomon said, *"The race is not to the swift"* (Ecclesiastes 9:11). It's about those who endure to the end and finish their course. It may look like you'll never finish what God called you to do. It may look like you'll never be the best. That's why you have to keep your eyes on Jesus. Your flesh will want to take a shortcut and run in the lane of another. Don't do that, regardless of how slow your race seems.

This race is all about faith in God. It's not important how fast you run it. It is crucial that you simply refuse to quit believing that God has a plan that He's working out in your life. It may be over the next hill, or you may not see it for a while, but keep running.

Keep believing.

Keep the faith.

Good runners remove everything that will weigh them down. They take the ankle weights off their feet. They remove heavy, bulky clothing. They start to strip down. They don't want anything to encumber them.

Since we have such a huge crowd of men of faith watching us from the grandstands, let us strip off anything that slows us down or holds us back, and especially those sins that wrap themselves so tightly around our feet and trip us up; and let us run with patience the particular race that God has set before us. Keep your eyes on Jesus, our leader and instructor. (Hebrews 12:1–2 TLB)

Or, as it says in the the *New King James Version*:

Therefore we also, since we are surrounded by so great a cloud of witnesses, let us lay aside every weight, and the sin which so easily ensnares us, and let us run with endurance the race that is set before us, looking unto Jesus, the author and finisher of our faith.

Strip away the sin from your life. You know what it is and so does God. Unshackle yourself from the way sin has wrapped itself around your life. You can't finish your race dragging it along behind you. Be quick to repent and turn from sin. Whenever it attempts to trip you, strip it away through repentance. Stay diligent to stand against it.

But understand that some of the weights that drag you down are not your sin. Sometimes other people weigh you down. They may be friends or relatives who have their own agenda for your life. You had better learn to strip them away. You'll have to let them go and loosen yourself from their grasp.

When I first began running my race to fulfill God's purpose in my life, I realized there were some things I couldn't carry onto the track. I had to let go of my family: my mother, dad, brother, and sister. I loved them, and they didn't mean me any harm. But sometimes those who love us will do anything to protect us from disappointment. And in order to avoid disappointment, they will try to influence us to take the easy road where we will be safe.

I had to let go of friends and coworkers who weren't cheering me on, but were weighing me down. They were just dead weight, and I couldn't finish my course with them hanging their expectations on me. I had to focus on Jesus, and the fact that He would help me finish my course. I had to think about the new thing Jesus was doing in me. I had to remind myself that He would be faithful to finish what He began. I learned that you can never become the best until you make the decision to finish.

Character: The Characteristic of a Winner

There is a difference between the "old you" and the "new you." That difference is the character that Jesus is forming in you. It is the difference between you and the world. It is the difference between the believer and the nonbeliever.

I'm not saying that all nonbelievers lack character. I'm just saying that God's character isn't being formed in them. God's character is the best, and that's what is being formed in you.

You'll need God's character to finish your course. You'll need it to endure. You'll need it to stay in your lane. You'll need it to resist taking shortcuts through another runner's race. You'll need it when you're far behind the pack, and it doesn't look like you'll ever finish. You'll need it to keep from giving up. You'll need it because it will bring patience.

So, since we have been made right in God's sight by faith in His promises, we can have real peace with Him because of what Jesus Christ our Lord has done for us. Because of our faith, he has brought us into this place of highest privilege where we now stand, and we confidently and joyfully look forward to actually becoming all that God has had in mind for us to be.

> So now, since we have been made right in God's sight by faith in his promises, we can have real peace with him because of what Jesus Christ our Lord has done for us. For because of our faith, he has brought us into this place of highest privilege where we now stand, and we confidently and joyfully look forward to actually becoming all that God has had in mind for us to be. We can rejoice, too, when we run into problems and trials, for we know that they are good for us—they help us learn to be patient. And patience develops strength of character in us and helps us trust God more each time we use it until finally our hope and faith are strong and steady. (Romans 5:1-4 TLB)

Tests, trials, hardships, suffering, problems, and persecutions are guaranteed in this race toward the high calling of God's purpose for our lives. Yet James told us to count it all joy when we fall into fiery trials, tests, and tribulations. (See James 1:2.)

In other words, you'll face hurdles along the way. You'll jump over most of them, but you may have to crawl under a few. You might get knocked down, but you have to get up and keep going. You have to keep your eyes on Jesus and count it joy, because you know that the process is working patience in you.

God wants you on the other side of the hurdle that is in your path. It is God's character that keeps you in the race. It is patience that keeps you going. It is faith that says, "I'm tired. I don't really know where I'm going, but I know I'm going on with God. I will not stop. I will not turn back. I will finish."

God's plan is for you to develop the mind of Christ. It is consistent: the same yesterday, today, and forever. It is a characteristic of God. It teaches you to not be moved by what you see. You are not moved by what you feel. You are not moved by what you hear. You are moved by the Spirit of the Living God.

A good example of God's character is a statue. Think about the Statue of Liberty. It stands in New York harbor and represents freedom, independence, and liberty. It was the same yesterday as it is today. It doesn't change when storms hit. It isn't moved by the wind. It doesn't sway or budge.

God is looking for people who have that kind of character. They have the sword of the Spirit in one hand, and the praise of God in their mouths. It doesn't matter what the devil throws at them; they constantly stand for God.

The world loves people of character. That's why the world loved John Wayne. He may have been in different kinds of movies, but he always played roles of the same kind of character.

Mohammad Ali was the same way. He was always "the greatest." If he got beat up, he stayed the same. He still said, "I'm the greatest!" He didn't change.

The world is looking for people of character—people like Martin Luther King and Gandhi. Talent will only entertain;

character will endure. A lot of athletes are paid multimillion-dollar contracts. They have talent—but many have little to no character.

Too many Christians would rather be entertained in church than become a person of character. God has given you talent, but He desires to take you to a whole new level called character.

> God has given you talent, but He desires to take you to a whole new level called character.

Herein is our love made perfect, that we may have boldness in the day of judgment: because as he is, so are we in this world. (1 John 4:17 KJV)

The world loves character. The world hungers for character. That's why God is developing His character in you. So the world will find Him in you.

When are you in the world? Now!

When are you to be like Jesus? Now!

You didn't feel like Jesus when you got up this morning. You didn't feel like Jesus in your car on your way to work today. But I'm letting you know that, right now, you can be like He is. That is your destiny.

Do you want to know what Jesus did?

And you no doubt know that Jesus of Nazareth was anointed by God with the Holy Spirit and with power, and he went around doing good and healing all who were possessed by demons, for God was with him. (Acts 10:38 TLB)

Do you want to know what you are supposed to be doing? You are to go about doing good to others. Your assignment is to finish what Jesus started. When you do that, your life will have meaning.

The graveyard is full of potential success and unfulfilled dreams and purposes. Jesus made an incredible statement before He died. He said, *"It is finished"* (John 19:30). Before Paul died he said, *"I have finished my course"* (2 Timothy 4:7 KJV). That's why the Bible says, *"O death, where is thy sting?"* (1 Corinthians 15:55).

> *For our earthly bodies, the ones we have now that can die, must be transformed into heavenly bodies that cannot perish but will live forever. When this happens, then at last this Scripture will come true—"Death is swallowed up in victory." O death, where then your victory? Where then your sting? For sin—the sting that causes death—will all be gone; and the law, which reveals our sins, will no longer be our judge. How we thank God for all of this! It is he who makes us victorious through Jesus Christ our Lord! So, my dear brothers, since future victory is sure, be strong and steady, always abounding in the Lord's work, for you know that nothing you do for the Lord is ever wasted as it would be if there were no resurrection.* (verses 53–58 TLB)

There is no sting in death when you have finished your race and fulfilled the call of God on your life. Death is truly swallowed up in victory.

CONFESSION:

Father, forgive me for the times I've wandered around, wondering what race to run, without ever asking You. Forgive me for trying to be the author and finisher of my own faith. Please set me on my course and help me stay in my lane. Above all, help me to not just begin my race, but to finish it well.

FAITH KEY #13—FINISH YOUR RACE

Do you know the race you are called to run? If not, stop and spend time alone with God in prayer. And don't forget the most important part: listening.

"Be still, and know that I am God" (Psalm 46:10).

Have you made a good start and stayed in your lane?

Make a firm commitment to finish.

"The race is not to the swift" (Ecclesiastes 9:11).

Key #14

MAKE YOUR LIFE A DONATION

Life Is Measured by Your Donation, Not by Your Duration

One of the Hebrew patriarchs mentioned in Genesis 5 was a man named Methuselah. Methuselah, a descendent of Seth, lived an amazing nine hundred sixty-nine years. There is no record of any other man living as long as Methuselah. Yet in all those years on earth, the Bible does not record a single thing that Methuselah ever did for God. He lived a long time—that's it.

Long life, in and of itself, means nothing. It doesn't mean you finished your course. It doesn't mean you satisfied yourself or God. It could mean that God gave you a lot of years to carry out His purpose on earth, and you still missed what He called you to do.

Living a long time doesn't mean anything because life is not measured by duration, but by donation. It's what you donate to the world that matters.

You may ask, "What if I don't have anything to offer?"

Offer whatever God has put in your hand—and God has given something to everyone.

Think about David, a shepherd boy destined to be a king. God put a slingshot in his hand long before He gave him a scepter. When he saw the giant, David declared, *"You come to me with a sword, with a spear, and with a javelin. But I come to you in the name of the LORD of hosts, the God of the armies of Israel, whom you have defied"* (1 Samuel 17:45).

> God has given something to everyone. Offer what God has put in your hand.

The first thing the world tried to do was take away the small weapon in David's hand, a slingshot, and give him something better: a sword and body armor. But David took them off, knowing that all he needed was already in his hands. (See verses 38–40.) He used what was in his hands to protect Israel and defend the name of the Lord. With one slingshot and five smooth stones, he killed the giant and routed the enemies of Israel.

The same thing happened to Moses. God said, in effect, "Moses, I want you to deliver all My people out of Egypt." Moses basically replied, "Who am I? There's nothing I can do!"

So the LORD said to [Moses], "What is that in your hand?" He said, "A rod." And He said, "Cast it on the ground." So he cast it on the ground, and it became a serpent.

(Exodus 4:2–3)

105

The amazing part of that miracle wasn't the rod as much as the ground he threw it on. It was holy ground. You have to make sure you sow your seed in holy ground, because that's where it will produce miraculous fruit.

YOU'RE BEING WATCHED

Never fear, God has already put in your hand everything you need for your future. What you have in your hand today may not be anything more spiritual than a slingshot or a rod. Whatever it is, dedicate it to God. Dedicate whatever is left of your life to Him. And never forget—you are being watched.

What do I mean by that? The Bible tells us that Jesus used to go to the temple and watch what people gave. Even today, Jesus is still the High Priest who watches over what each person gives. He is watching what you give in your life. He is also watching what you give of your life.

Now Jesus sat opposite the treasury and saw how the people put money into the treasury. And many who were rich put in much. Then one poor widow came and threw in two mites, which make a quadrans. So He called His disciples to Himself and said to them, "Assuredly, I say to you that this poor widow has put in more than all those who have given to the treasury; for they all put in out of their abundance, but she out of her poverty put in all that she had, her whole liveli-hood." (Mark 12:41–44)

Jesus was never as impressed with the quantity of the gift as He was with the quality of the gift. For instance, most ministries today are impressed with huge offerings that are often given out of great abundance. While those are a blessing, Jesus said that the widow who gave two mites gave more than all the others. A billionaire who gives millions can never outgive that widow who gave everything she owned.

The same is true of your life. Proverbs 18:16 says *"a man's gift makes room for him, and brings him before great men."* Each of us is given special talents and abilities. Whatever God has put in your hand isn't a gift—until it's given away.

CONFESSION:

> Father, I desire to make my life a donation. Open my eyes to see what You've put in my hands. Show me how to give it, and my life, to You and to the world. I ask this in Jesus' name, Amen.

FAITH KEY #14— MAKE YOUR LIFE A DONATION

Look back over your life to date. Is it marked more by duration or donation?

Think of the talents, gifts, and anointing God has given you. How have you given them away? How can you give more of them, making your life a donation?

> *Every good gift and every perfect gift is from above, and comes down from the Father of lights, with whom there is no variation or shadow of turning.* (James 1:17)

BUILD BRIDGES

Loneliness Comes to Those Who Build Walls— Not Bridges

The first step to salvation is recognizing that there are some things you can't do by yourself. You can't make it to heaven alone: that's why God sent Jesus. You need a relationship with Jesus, the greatest bridge builder in the world. He bridged the gap between God and all mankind. Jesus never builds walls. He is forever—yesterday, today, and tomorrow—building bridges. If you are born again, Jesus is calling you to build bridges, too.

But the enemy of your soul, the devil, is calling on your flesh to build walls. Walls are used to lock things in and to keep people out. You cannot continue to build walls and become the best. God isn't going to make you the best at anything just so you can be the best for yourself. You can only be the best if everyone else is able to see and appreciate what God is doing in your life.

Michael Jordan always had it in him to become the best basketball player. But none of us knew it until he got into a position where everyone could see for themselves that he was the best. People had to watch him and compare what he did with how others played the game. As long as he played alone in the gym, he was not the best.

Like Michael Jordan, you have the ability to become the best at what God has gifted you to do. But it won't happen until you come out from behind the walls that hide you. You have to break them down and start building bridges to other people.

The world teaches us to build up borders. When you buy a new house, the first thing you want to find is your property line. Then you put up a fence to keep your stuff in and other people out. Folks don't want your tree limbs hanging in their yard. They don't want to rake up your leaves. If you keep building up your borders, eventually they will be used to keep certain people out of your neighborhood because they might bring down the value of your home.

> God isn't going to make you the best at anything just so you can be the best for yourself.

As long as you have that mentality, violence will come within your borders. Waste will be found within the confines of your walls. And you'll be lonely.

The only solution to that problem is building bridges.

I will exchange your brass for gold, your iron for silver, your wood for brass, your stones for iron. Peace and righteousness shall be your taskmasters! Violence will disappear out of your land—all war will end. Your walls will be "Salvation" and your gates "Praise." (Isaiah 60:17–18 TLB)

If you continue to build walls, heaven will become brass to you, and the ground like iron. You will not get a harvest from heaven or earth. But God rewards bridge builders. The Bible says that when you build bridges, your walls will be called "Salvation" and your gates, "Praise." God will take away the brass and bring you gold. He will replace your wood, brass, and iron with silver. He will bring prosperity, peace, and righteousness to your borders.

PUTTING UP WALLS

You will need the Spirit of God to build bridges. Building walls is easy; all you need is flesh. You were born with the ability to build walls.

I was a master wall builder. Everything in my countenance screamed, "Stay away from me! Just leave me alone!" All I had was me, myself, and I. It was a lonely place to live. You can't even let God inside, because God will build bridges. We have churches today that don't let God inside. They want to be by themselves with their programs and agendas.

That's how cults begin—one wall at a time. Walls are crucial to every cult. Cults believe that only those inside can have God's best. If you ever get involved with an organization where people aren't free to come and go as they please, chances are you're involved in a cult.

That's not the way God operates. God gives His people hinds' feet, to leap over walls. (See Psalm 18:33.) He gives us spiritual power to pull down the strongholds that divide and separate. God builds bridges that allow everyone access. Bridges allow people to freely go in and out. In God, there is freedom and liberty.

DON'T JUDGE THE PEOPLE GOD SENDS OVER YOUR BRIDGE

For some time, the Lord had put it on my heart to start my own business. But I was a lot like Moses—I couldn't talk. So I wasted quite a bit of time arguing with God. He was telling me what He wanted me to do, but I was too busy concentrating on my weaknesses. I told myself that I needed confirmation that this crazy dream was really from God.

Then God put a name in my head: Jerry Wright. This was to be the one who would stand with me and speak for me. Now Jerry was a good friend, but he knew less about business than I did. For that reason I decided that this must not have been from God. But God refused to let up.

I remember the day I was walking toward my office and having a conversation with the Lord, trying to get out of His call. I finally decided to throw out a fleece. I know you're not supposed to do that with God, but I was really trying to get out of this thing. So I bargained with God, "If Jerry is really the one, have him call me up and ask me to go to lunch with him. And to confirm that this is really from you, have him invite me to go get soup for lunch."

Sure enough, later that day Jerry calls me and asks me to go to lunch. I almost told him that I brought my lunch but I was curious, so I went with him.

As we walked to lunch, Jerry was his normal, jovial self. But then Jerry stopped and said, "Why don't we just get soup today? I know this great place that just serves soup."

Now I was getting a little nervous.

We went to the restaurant and Jerry ordered soup. He asked me what kind of soup I wanted and what kind of bread I wanted—honestly, I didn't know. I was too blown away by what God was doing to worry about what soup to get.

When we finally sat down to eat soup, Jerry was talking about everything under the sun. I was literally sitting there trembling because I now knew that God had spoken to me.

I decided that I would share my dream of starting a business with Jerry, but if he thought I was crazy, then he wouldn't be the one. So I shared my dream and Jerry jumped up from his chair and cried out, "Yes! Yes! When can we start?"

That's how God started my business, and that's how Jerry Wright became my partner. At that point I decided that maybe God was talking to me.

Just as I was an unlikely person for God to call to starting a consulting business, Jerry was not the person I would have chosen to go into business with. Nobody would have picked Jerry. But God did. If I hadn't let down my wall and built a bridge to Jerry, none of it would have happened.

A BRIDGE TO GRACE

I get excited when I think about Christians walking around as shining examples of God's best in the world. When you let the walls fall down, the floodgates of God's favor will overtake you. You may have justified building walls by saying you were protecting the anointing. The simple truth is that you haven't protected anything except your loneliness.

There are two things you need in order to become God's best. You need charisma and you need love. The word *charisma* comes from the word *charis*, which is our word for *grace*. It means "to be empowered or anointed to do." When charisma comes into your life, the Spirit of God is upon you to enable you to do whatever He has called you to do. When that happens, people say, "Oh, he's anointed!" They don't say, "Oh, he's graced." When great grace is upon someone, that person is anointed. So you must have the anointing of God, which comes through His grace.

I must warn you though: it does no good to have that anointing on your life if you're not willing to share His empowering presence with others. Don't build walls around God's empowering presence in your life. If no one can see that you're a Christian, what good is that?

CONFESSION:

> Father, forgive me for building walls around the parts of my life that I don't want anyone—including You— to enter. I ask that Your anointing would destroy the walls my fear and flesh have built. Show me the walls in my life that I don't see. Teach me and empower me to build bridges into Your kingdom.

FAITH KEY #15—BUILD BRIDGES

Take the time to think about what walls you may have unknowingly built in your life. Repent for building them and let them fall.

How can you build bridges between yourself and others? Only by faith:

> *By faith the walls of Jericho fell down after they were encircled for seven days.*   (Hebrews 11:30)

Key #16

SURRENDER

The Greatest Strength Is in Total Surrender to God

In 2 Corinthians 12, we find the apostle Paul pleading with the Lord over a particular situation. Many people have misunderstood this passage, thinking it meant that God desired Paul to live with sickness. That is far from the truth! Let's look at God's response in order to see the truth.

The word *grace* here is the word you commonly use as "being empowered" or "anointed."

> *Concerning this thing I pleaded with the Lord three times that it might depart from me. And He said to me, "My grace is sufficient for you, for My strength is made perfect in weakness." Therefore most gladly I will rather boast in my infirmities, that the power of Christ may rest upon me. Therefore I take pleasure in infirmities, in reproaches, in needs, in persecutions, in distresses, for Christ's sake. For when I am weak, then I am strong.* (2 Corinthians 12:8–10)

God didn't tell Paul to be patient. He said, *"My grace* [anointing] *is sufficient for you."* But in order for Paul to receive that anointing, he had to do something. What was it?

He had to surrender.

The best relationship you can have with God is one of surrender.

"But Lord, no..."

Surrender.

"God, I can't!"

Surrender.

"If only...."

Surrender.

If you want the anointing of God, you must surrender. Your flesh is an enemy to God. Your words, unless anointed, are an enemy to God. Your thoughts and attitudes have been trained by the world system.

Surrender means, "I give up! I've tried to do this on my own, but it didn't work. So now I give up." "I've been trying to work things out my way, but now I'm going to stop trying so hard. I'm just going to surrender."

That's what Paul said. "Lord, I tried to deal with this thing three times. I even prayed about it three times. I tried to get rid of it a thousand times on my own, but it wouldn't go."

The Lord said, "My anointing is enough—stop trying so hard!"

He's saying the same thing to you today: "Will you stop trying so hard?"

You might respond, "But you don't understand my shortcomings!"

I didn't say to ignore your shortcomings. I said surrender them. That's all He's asking you to do. Have you ever wondered how Paul could say, *"I take pleasure in infirmities* [weakness]" (2 Corinthians 12:10)? It's because every time he saw his own weakness, he knew God would step into that area and become strong!

This is the power of the gospel: Where you are weak, God becomes strong. But it only happens through surrender—just letting it go. Without surrender, you are missing a major key to your personal and professional success.

> This is the power of the gospel: When you are weak, God is strong.

Instead of surrender, most Christians just give up.

Surrender is the polar opposite of giving up!

SURRENDER YOUR WEAKNESS

Let's say you're weak in the area of finances, but you haven't surrendered it to God. Instead, you've tried everything you know to do in your own power, and nothing has improved. In fact, your financial picture looks bleaker than it looked before! When opportunity comes knocking at your door, you refuse to answer. This is how you sound:

"I can't get an education!"

"I can't buy my own home!"

"I can't build a building!"

"I can't afford a vacation."

"I can't buy land."

"I can't give into the building fund."

"I can't get ahead."

You've given up on what you can do, but in the process you've also given up on God!

If you want to find the key to personal and professional success, you must begin by repenting for the ways in which you have limited God. Then tell Him that you are weak in the area of your finances and surrender it to Him. Stop trying so hard to get ahead, and start trusting God to move into your situation.

> *Cast your burden on the LORD, And He shall sustain you.*
> (Psalm 55:22)

Trust Him so much that you will only speak what God has to say about your situation:

"I believe that God will make a way where there seems to be no way!"

"I'm trusting God to help me buy my own home."

"The favor of the Lord is on me to cause me to succeed in my career."

> *The blessing of the LORD makes one rich, and He adds no sorrow with it.* (Proverbs 10:22)

> *Give, and it will be given to you: good measure, pressed down, shaken together, and running over.* (Luke 6:38)

> *My God shall supply all your need according to His riches in glory by Christ Jesus.* (Philippians 4:19)

> *They overcame him by the blood of the Lamb and by the word of their testimony.* (Revelation 12:11)

It doesn't matter what your weakness is. You may be weak in the area of pornography; you may have tried to kick that habit out of the solar system, but it continues to lift its ugly head. Surrender!

When you learn to let go and surrender, something amazing happens. Every time you confront a situation where you can't do something, instead of getting into doubt and despair, you'll get excited. Why? Because you'll know that you've surrendered that area of your life to God, and that means He's going to show Himself strong.

To obtain this key to opening the door to your future, you must constantly ask yourself these questions:

Whose report will I believe?

Will I believe circumstances that scream at me day after day?

Or will I believe the Word of God?

How you answer those questions will determine how you will live the rest of your life.

I know what it means to be limited in life. Limitations defined my life for years until I got tired of living in a box. It's lonely behind those walls! When I got the revelation that God would be my strength, I decided to become the best that I could be.

On the football field, I realized I relied on a coach to push me; I could motivate myself. I went far beyond what the coach asked of me! I moved into a different realm—a whole different zone.

I moved into the "God Zone," and I have to tell you— it's the only way to live! Living in the God Zone is like being plugged into power and purpose.

It makes waking up each morning an exciting adventure.

CONFESSION:

Father, I want to live in the God Zone! Help me surrender all my weaknesses to You! By faith I release them now and let them go. Help me learn, once and for all, that I cannot win a spiritual victory in my own strength. Amen.

FAITH KEY #16—LETTING GO

Spend time in the presence of the Lord and surrender your weaknesses to Him. Resist the temptation to pick them up. Let go. Let God.

For though He was crucified in weakness, yet He lives by the power of God. For we also are weak in Him, but we shall live with Him by the power of God toward you.

(2 Corinthians 13:4)

Key #17

THE SECRET TO SUCCESS

Whatever Good You Do for Others
You Will Receive from the Lord

There is another principle that you can tap into in order to move into the God Zone. This principle is one of the most overlooked principles in the Bible. It is another key to your victorious life:

Knowing that whatever good anyone does, he will receive the same from the Lord, whether he is a slave or free.

(Ephesians 6:8)

This principle points to a new realm in God, and involves the Law of Love. In essence, this Scripture makes it clear that you cannot succeed alone.

God never intended anyone to succeed alone. In the garden of Eden, the Lord created Eve because He knew it was not good for Adam to live alone. That's precisely why the devil will entice you to build walls around yourself—he knows it will keep you from the success God has planned for you.

To move into the God Zone, you must recognize that you cannot be alone.

You cannot get there by building walls.

You must build godly relationships.

It's the same reason that the law of love must be in operation to have a successful marriage. It's the same reason that no one can have a family by themselves. It's the same reason that God sent Jesus. We can not make it to heaven alone.

We must have a relationship with Jesus.

The law of love in operation always brings success.

THE SECRET OF SUCCESS

Ephesians 6:8 is the secret to success. It simply says, in effect, "Whatever you make happen to others, God will make happen for you."

The power is in your hands.

When you understand this principle, you will knock down every wall that surrounds you and come out blasting. You will look for someone to bless. When you go to work, you will be determined to make your boss a success. You will do whatever it takes, legitimately, to make your supervisor successful. It won't matter to you if the man is good or bad. You don't have to worry about that because if he gets his promotion, God will turn around and make sure you get yours.

> Scripture makes it clear that you cannot succeed alone.

A revelation of Ephesians 6:8 will stop all the backbiting and gossip. Your attitude will be, "I'm here to serve you." You'll work overtime to make sure your supervisor, who has passed you over for every promotion, wins the Employee of the Month award. It won't matter if your boss despises you and opposes everything you do. When you learn the secret of success, you will look for ways to bless him. Jesus told us how to treat those who oppose us:

> *Love your enemies, bless those who curse you, do good to those who hate you, and pray for those who spitefully use you and persecute you, that you may be sons of your Father in heaven.* (Matthew 5:44–45).

Everything you get from God begins as a seed. If you want a successful marriage, start doing everything in your power to make your spouse the most successful person they can be. Help them fulfill their deepest desires and dreams. Whatever you want, help someone else get it.

You don't have to look far and wide, just turn to the people God has put in your path. Because God is going to bless you in the same way that you bless other people.

This is God's promise to you in Ephesians 6:8, and God will always fulfill His Word. If you want a biblical example of this principle, remember Job. Great disaster fell on Job. He lost all of his children. He lost all of his cattle and flocks. He lost all of his wealth. He lost his health. The only thing Job had left was his life, a nagging wife, and friends who persecuted and accused him.

But in the midst of this tragedy, Job grabbed hold of this principle. When he did, he decided to tear down every bridge in his life. He had nothing left to give except the greatest gift of all—prayer. The Bible says that Job prayed for his friends:

Then all his brothers, all his sisters, and all those who had been his acquaintances before, came to him and ate food with him in his house; and they consoled him and comforted him for all the adversity that the LORD had brought upon him. Each one gave him a piece of silver and each a ring of gold. Now the LORD blessed the latter days of Job more than his beginning; for he had fourteen thousand sheep, six thousand camels, one thousand yoke of oxen, and one thousand female donkeys. He also had seven sons and three daughters. And he called the name of the first Jemimah, the name of the second Keziah, and the name of the third Keren-Happuch. In all the land were found no women so beautiful as the daughters of Job; and their father gave them an inheritance among their brothers. After this Job lived one hundred and forty years, and saw his children and grandchildren for four generations. So Job died, old and full of days. (Job 42:11–17)

Jesus taught a great deal about this secret of success as well. In Matthew, He said,

You have heard that it was said, "You shall love your neighbor and hate your enemy." But I say to you, love your enemies, bless those who curse you, do good to those who hate you, and pray for those who spitefully use you and persecute you, that you may be sons of your Father in heaven; for He makes His sun rise on the evil and on the good, and sends rain on the just and on the unjust. For if you love those who love you, what reward have you? (Matthew 5:43–46)

Jesus not only taught it, He lived it, suffering the shame of death by crucifixion so that you would not pay the price for your sin. He gave you life.

It is up to you what you do with it.

Why not make the most of it?

Live it in the God Zone.

CONFESSION:

Father, I desire to move into the God Zone. Please, open my eyes to ways I can bless and promote other people. Help me not only to learn, but to live, the secret to success. Amen.

FAITH KEY #17—THE SECRET TO SUCCESS

If you want to receive a double portion from God, the first step is to give the greatest gift—prayer. Make a list of your friends, and include the people who have hurt you, persecuted you, or oppressed you. Pray for them, fervently, every day, asking God to give them a double portion of blessing.

Look for ways to help other people get exactly what you desire. Bless someone in this way every single day.

And the LORD restored Job's losses when he prayed for his friends. Indeed the LORD gave Job twice as much as he had before. (Job 42:10)

Key #18

MEDITATION

Meditation Incubates Your Faith

This is the most important key to personal and professional success. In fact, this principle is so vital that it is virtually impossible to live victoriously without it. Yet I would hazard to guess that most Christians stumble because they lack this crucial key.

Consider one of the greatest times in human history, when Moses led the Israelites out of bondage in Egypt. The Bible says that God spoke to Moses face-to-face, as with a friend. The glory of God descended with such awesome power that Moses had to cover his face because it glowed. Yet when those meetings between God and Moses were finished and Moses returned to his tent, one man stayed, lingering in the presence of God. (See Exodus 33:11.)

That man was Joshua, son of Nun, Moses' assistant. Joshua had a hunger for God greater than anyone else in the camp. While everyone else slept, Joshua worshipped at the tent of meeting. No wonder God chose him as Moses' successor. No wonder he was elected to lead the Israelites out of the wilderness and into the Promised Land. It was Joshua who crossed the Jordan. It was Joshua who led Israel in her silent march around the walls of Jericho until they brought the walls tumbling down with a shout. It was Joshua who led the Israelite army into battle and won their inheritance.

Joshua conquered huge obstacles to live a magnificently victorious life. How did he overcome such odds? It may have been in the twilight hours, as Joshua worshipped the Lord, that God revealed to him the greatest key to success.

> *This Book of the Law shall not depart from your mouth, but you shall meditate in it day and night, that you may observe to do according to all that is written in it. For then you will make your way prosperous, and then you will have good success.* (Joshua 1:8)

God's promise of success was conditional. First, you have to meditate on God's law day and night. This promise wasn't fulfilled by meditating on God's law on Sunday mornings. It wasn't fulfilled by meditating on God's law during midweek services, or at home fellowship group. It wasn't even fulfilled by meditating on God's law once a day. No, for success, God required Joshua to meditate on it day and night. In other words, Joshua couldn't let the Word of God depart from his thoughts or his mouth.

> Your task is to move God's Word from your spirit to your mind, will, and emotions.

Joshua did these things, and then God made him prosperous and successful.

God requires no less of you today.

126

FAITH COMES BY HEARING

I know that's not what you want to hear, but it's the truth. Today, many Christians never meditate on God's Word. They don't ponder it and mutter it. They don't talk about it night and day. They don't allow themselves to become consumed with it. They don't teach it to their children when they get up and when they go to bed.

If the walls of your Jericho are going to fall, you've got to do exactly what Joshua did. You've got to meditate on God's Word day and night, refusing to let it depart from your thoughts or your mouth.

To understand how this works, remember that you are made in God's image. You have a spirit, you have a soul, and you live in a body. The part of you that most people mistakenly think is the real you is your body. Your body functions as a "space suit." It allows you to survive on this planet. If you lose your body, you have to leave earth.

The Word of God builds up your spirit—the real you, made in God's image. Your task is to move God's Word from your spirit into your soul, which is made up of your mind, will, and emotions. This is called renewing your mind. It changes the way you think, the way you feel, and the way you act.

That's what meditation does. It builds your spirit and changes your soul, which in turn can heal your body. Everything you do in life requires faith. The Bible says that faith comes by hearing, and hearing by the Word of God. That's how it gets in you to affect your spirit, renew your soul, and heal your body. In other words, meditation incubates your faith.

SEED FAITH

You've probably seen a premature baby. Their little lungs are often underdeveloped. They aren't developed enough to survive outside their mother's womb. Without medical intervention, many of them would die soon after birth. But scientists have created an artificial environment, much like their mother's womb, where premature babies can grow and continue to develop. That environment is called an incubator.

The Bible says that the Word of God is a seed in you. It has to be protected, nurtured, and developed. That's what meditation does. It is the incubator that creates the environment for your faith to survive and grow. In other words, faith does not drop into you in full-grown maturity—it must incubate.

Think about an apple seed. Does it allow you to eat a whole apple? No, a seed must be planted in good ground. It must germinate. It must be allowed to grow into a tree. The tree has to grow branches and leaves. In time, it will produce fruit.

The same is true of your faith. That may be why Jesus said that if you understand the parable of the seed, you will understand all parables. The Word of God becomes a seed of faith inside of you. It will never produce victorious living unless it's incubated and allowed to develop into a full-grown tree, which produces good fruit.

THE SPIRIT OF FAITH

So, why do you hear so many Christians spouting their confessions of faith that never come true? It's because they speak too soon.

We have the same spirit of faith, according to what is written, "I believed and therefore I spoke," we also believe and therefore speak. (2 Corinthians 4:13)

Most Christians try to work this spiritual law backwards. They speak, hoping that if they say something often enough they'll start believing it.

The spirit of faith doesn't work that way. That's why people have labeled it, "Name it and claim it" or "Blab it and grab it." Call it what you will, faith doesn't work that way. A lot of people hear what the preacher says, and then they turn around and say the same thing. The difference is that they're just parroting something someone else believed. They don't believe it. Yet they keep saying it over and over and finally give up with, "This faith stuff doesn't work!"

The key is to believe before you speak. How do you believe something you've never experienced? You have to incubate your faith by meditating on God's promises.

God responds to us by our faith. Scripture says, *"Without faith it is impossible to please Him"* (Hebrews 11:6). However, we don't all have identical faith. What's the difference? The reason you see some victorious believers with full-grown faith and others with weak little faith seedlings is because full-grown faith has been incubated through meditation on God's Word.

Let's take another look at the key for success that God taught Joshua:

This Book of the Law shall not depart from your mouth, but you shall meditate in it day and night, that you may observe to do according to all that is written in it. For then you will make your way prosperous, and then you will have good success. (Joshua 1:8)

According to this passage, God's promise of prosperity and success hinges on three things we must do: (1) never let God's law depart from your mouth; (2) talk about it; (3) meditate on God's law day and night.

This requires consistency.

When you meditate on the Word day and night, talk about the Word day and night, and do what it says, then God will cause the walls of your Jericho to fall.

You are on your way to personal and professional success.

CONFESSION:

> Father, I desire the same spirit of faith that Joshua had. I know that means I need to incubate my faith the way he incubated his. Help me to make meditating on Your Word the light that I live by. I choose to meditate on Your Word, talk about Your Word, and obey Your Word. I ask that, like Joshua, You teach me Your ways even as I praise Your holy name. Amen.

FAITH KEY #18—RATE, THEN INCUBATE

How would you describe your faith? Is it a seed that has withered and dried from lack of care? Is it a seedling that must be in the proper environment to grow? Is God's Word the first thing you think of each morning and your last thought each night? Do you have full-grown faith for healing, but a seedling faith where prosperity is concerned?

Rate your faith...then incubate!

Tips for meditating on God's Word:

(1) Read the *One Year Bible* through each year in a different version. Every day you'll read from the Old Testament, New Testament, Psalms, and Proverbs.

(2) Keep the Bible on tape or teaching tapes in your bathroom, bedroom, kitchen, and car. Play them daily.

(3) Wear a CD or MP3 player during your walk or work-out at the gym. Allow the Word of God to strengthen your spirit while you strengthen your body.

(4) Buy Scripture confession books, or make your own list and tape it to your bathroom mirror. Speak the Word; don't let it depart from your mouth.

Blessed is the man who walks not in the counsel of the ungodly, nor stands in the path of sinners, nor sits in the seat of the scornful; but his delight is in the law of the LORD, and in His law he meditates day and night. He shall be like a tree planted by the rivers of water, that brings forth its fruit in its season, whose leaf also shall not wither; and whatever he does shall prosper. (Psalm 1:1–3)

Key #19

JUST IMAGINE

Within Your Imagination Is the Power to Create

I f you're going to live a successful life in Christ Jesus, it's imperative that you know how to communicate with God. We've already discussed that the primary way you receive wisdom and instructions from Him is through His Word. The Lord will never tell you anything that is contrary to His written Word. So the Bible must be what anchors your soul. It must be the standard by which everything in your life is tested.

Another common way the Lord speaks is through dreams and visions. In many cases, the Holy Spirit has been trying to talk to you, but you haven't known how to receive and interpret His communication. That's because dreams and visions operate through your imagination, which the world and the devil have perverted.

Right now, some of you are thinking, *Imagination? I thought we were going to learn about faith.*

132

That's exactly what we're talking about. Let's break down each component of faith and see how it works. That way, if you ever wreck your faith, you'll know how to put it back together. You'll know how all the pieces fit. You won't have to call someone to tow you into a garage. If you understand how faith works, you'll be able to make the necessary repairs yourself.

"You don't understand," you may say, "I'm falling apart over here."

Honestly, I understand all too well. I've heard the pitiful cries of real pain often enough.

"My husband is gone and I can't cope anymore!"

"My kids are on drugs and I don't know what to do!"

"I lost my job and I don't have any money!"

"Help me!"

I know you need help. You need to know how to open up the hood, look underneath, and figure out what's not working.

ABOVE AND NOT BENEATH

We'll start at the very beginning. Let's look at Genesis 1:26:

> Then God said, "Let Us make man in Our image, according to Our likeness; let them have dominion over the fish of the sea, over the birds of the air, and over the cattle, over all the earth and over every creeping thing that creeps on the earth."

I want you to notice that God has placed you over everything on earth—not under. God created you to be the first, not the last; the head and not the tail; above and not beneath. Your life should not be a reflection of what *you* can do; it should be a reflection of what *God* can do through you.

God said, *"Let's make man in Our image."* God created you in His image. The word *image* means "a carbon copy," "an imitation." A carbon copy isn't the original, but it's as close as you can get to the original.

The word *imagination* comes from the root word *image*. One of the definitions of *imagine* is "to meditate, ponder or consider." We've already discussed the vital role meditation plays in victorious living, but now you can see that your imagination is a key to meditation.

> God gave you an imagination in order to create a line of communication.

Another definition of *imagination* is "the power to create mental images from what has never been experienced or from what has never existed." Think about that for a moment. You have the power to create something out of nothing through your imagination.

God gave you an imagination in order to create a line of communication. Until now, you probably thought that communication was just talking. Granted, talking is a way to communicate, but it is the lowest form. For example, talking is not the highest form of communication between married couples. The highest form of communication occurs when no words are necessary. There are moments when a couple is so tuned into one another that words would spoil the moment.

The same is true in your communication with God. Speaking in tongues—as vital as it is—is not the highest form of communication. The Bible says that he who speaks in an unknown tongue speaks to God, even as others don't necessarily under-stand what was just said. (See 1 Corinthians 14:2–4.)

But the Holy Spirit speaks through dreams and visions, as well as through your imagination. If you are a believer, therefore, and yet you haven't been able to tap into what God is saying, it might be because someone else has tapped into you.

TAPPING INTO LINES OF COMMUNICATION

There is a war in the spirit over our ability to communi-cate with God. What is the first thing to happen when any war is declared? The enemy wants to break down lines of com-munication. Satan understands that your ability to hear from God puts his plans in peril. He knows he can't stop God from communicating, so he has decided to infiltrate, disrupt, and destroy your ability to hear from God.

In the garden of Eden, Adam and Eve could hear the voice of the Lord clearly. So how did Satan disrupt that communi-cation? He perverted Eve's imagination. He sparked a desire in her for something she didn't have—the forbidden fruit. A desire is a mental image of something you don't have. God told them they would die if they ate the fruit. (See Genesis 2:17.) Satan whispered, *"You will not surely die"* (Genesis 3:4).

So when the woman saw that the tree was good for food, that it was pleasant to the eyes, and a tree desirable to make one wise, she took of its fruit and ate. She also gave to her hus-band with her, and he ate. Then the eyes of both of them were opened, and they knew that they were naked; and they sewed fig leaves together and made themselves coverings. And they heard the sound of the LORD God walking in the garden in the cool of the day, and Adam and his wife hid themselves

135

*from the presence of the LORD God among the trees of the
garden.*   (Genesis 3:6–8)

The only way Satan could corrupt the line of communication between God and man was through Eve's imagination. He
convinced her to change her image of herself. She'd already
been made in the image of God. All he had to do was distort
the way she thought of herself.

Does that old trick sound familiar?

It worked in the garden of Eden, and it is still working to
this day.

STATIC ON THE LINE

What you are today is a result of how you've bought into
the world's image of you. The world has caused you to create,
with your own imagination, an image of yourself always falling
short of the greatness God programmed into you. That's why
you don't think that you can become the best at anything. That's
why you don't think you can get ahead. That's why you don't
think you can live in the 1 percent. You're constantly being
bombarded in your most vulnerable and powerful place—your
imagination.

The devil got Eve to think, *I could be like God!*

Once she enticed Adam to sin, all either of them could
hear was the devil. We see the result in Genesis 11:

*And the whole earth was of one language, and of one speech.
And it came to pass, as they journeyed from the east, that
they found a plain in the land of Shinar; and they dwelt
there. And they said one to another, Go to, let us make brick,
and burn them thoroughly. And they had brick for stone,
and slime had they for mortar. And they said, Go to, let*

us build us a city and a tower, whose top may reach unto heaven; and let us make us a name, lest we be scattered abroad upon the face of the whole earth. And the LORD came down to see the city and the tower, which the children of men builded. And the LORD said, Behold, the people is one, and they have all one language; and this they begin to do: and now nothing will be restrained from them, which they have imagined to do. (Genesis 11:1–6 KJV)

The devil had tempted them with his own sin: they wanted to be greater than God. Satan had taken over their imagination to the point that they were all in one accord, as the power of their imagination was working for evil.

BE TRANSFORMED

Just as he did in ancient Babylon, Satan has infiltrated our line of communication with God through our imagination. He perverts it with negative images through magazines, music, television, video games, books, movies, and the Internet.

Take music for instance. God created music and He gave it to us. Music creates an image. It motivates and moves us. That's why you dance; you can feel every note. You listen to a sad song, and you feel sad. It captures your imagination.

> Satan has infiltrated our line of communication with God through our imagination.

That's why the Bible says, *"Do not be conformed to this world, but be transformed by the renewing of your mind"* (Romans 12:2). God knew your mind would have to be renewed if you spent any time in this society.

Your imagination is key to the image you have of yourself. How do you get it back? Repent and give your imagination back to God. Meditate on the Word, and watch the Lord turn this thing around for you.

The Deceiver

Genesis 30 tells about a man named Jacob who was a forerunner of you. The word *Jacob* means "deceiver." That's what many of us in the body of Christ are doing. We love God but we deceive ourselves. How do you deceive yourself? You read the Word, you love the Lord, but you deceive yourself with your own image.

You might as well stand in the mirror and say, "Go ahead, hit me right here!" You're standing there defeating yourself. You're not defeated because of your background. You're not defeated because of your education, or lack of it. You're not defeated because of poverty.

You're defeated by what you have imagined about yourself. It doesn't matter if you live in the White House or the ghetto. We all have the same problem: we have lost our line of communication with God, and we have to get it back.

Jacob was a man who was blessed of God, but he always seemed to fail. He deceived his brother out of his birthright and had to run for his life. He imagined being married to Rachel, the youngest of his uncle Laban's daughters. He worked seven years for Rachel, but Laban was more of a deceiver than Jacob. Hidden behind the wedding veil wasn't Rachel; it was her older sister, Leah. Jacob worked yet another seven years for Rachel. He ended up with two wives and no money because Laban kept changing his salary.

Jacob had a failure mentality. That's where the devil had hooked into his imagination. It didn't matter how hard he worked, because he had already programmed himself to fail. Finally, he called out to God for help.

LET'S MAKE A DEAL

God knew that in order for Jacob to succeed, he'd have to change what he imagined. God said, in effect, "I want you to make a deal with Laban. When he offers you money, tell him you don't want any. Tell him you will work for free. Tell him all you ask for are the spotted goats."

Laban got excited and grabbed the deal. "I'll take all the white goats," he said. He understood some things about genetics and figured to get even richer off of Jacob.

Here's what God had Jacob do:

Now Jacob took for himself rods of green poplar and of the almond and chestnut trees, peeled white strips in them, and exposed the white which was in the rods. And the rods which he had peeled, he set before the flocks in the gutters, in the watering troughs where the flocks came to drink, so that they should conceive when they came to drink. So the flocks conceived before the rods, and the flocks brought forth streaked, speckled, and spotted. Then Jacob separated the lambs, and made the flocks face toward the streaked and all the brown in the flock of Laban; but he put his own flocks by themselves and did not put them with Laban's flock. And it came to pass, whenever the stronger livestock conceived, that Jacob placed the rods before the eyes of the livestock in the gutters, that they might conceive among the rods. But when the flocks were feeble, he did not put them in; so the feebler were Laban's and the stronger Jacob's. Thus the man

OPENING THE DOOR TO YOUR FUTURE

became exceedingly prosperous, and had large flocks, female and male servants, and camels and donkeys.

(Genesis 30:37–43)

SPOTTED GOATS

Jacob became the richest man around by placing speckled rods in the water when the flock was drinking. They would conceive spotted lambs. The goats weren't looking at the spots and saying, "Oh, I'm going to have spotted babies!"

Every time Jacob placed the spotted rods in the water it sparked his imagination. He no longer saw himself poor. He saw himself a rich man. He saw himself blessed with many spotted goats. He saw his kids running around in new shoes. He began to meditate on how rich he would become. He imagined himself prosperous. (See Genesis 31:10–16.)

He used his imagination as he meditated on the Word of God. The key to your success is meditation. The key to meditation is your imagination.

If you want to think about the power of imagination, look at The Disney Corporation. Disney has gone far beyond a corporation. They are almost a "nation." They create their own money, called "Disney dollars." They have their own places for you to stay. They provide your transportation. It's a mini-nation, and it all started with one man's imagination. Walt Disney looked at an orange grove in Florida and saw Disney World. He looked at a cartoon drawing of a mouse and saw an empire.

THE SEAT OF THE SOUL

For as he thinks in his heart, so is he. "Eat and drink!" he says to you, but his heart is not with you. (Proverbs 23:7)

140

This Proverb states that as a man thinks in his heart, *"so is he."* When you get up in the morning, you don't plan your day by thinking in your heart. You think with your conscious mind. Your heart is your unconscious mind. It's your subconscious, the place where dreams and visions take place.

Let's take a look at your mind. There are four elements to the mind:

Thought—Thoughts are the first element of your mind. Your thoughts are not always yours. You get suggestions from other people. You can also receive suggested thoughts from other beings—Satan can suggest thoughts, as can God.

Learning—The second element of your mind is the ability to learn. Right now you are learning. In other words, you are being trained.

Understanding—The third element of your mind is the ability to comprehend what you have learned. Comprehending brings understanding.

Imagination—The fourth element of your mind is your imagination. It is the imagination that allows you to leave the mental realm and enter the realm of the heart. You might say that your imagination opens the door to your heart—not your physical heart, but your spirit—where the Holy Spirit is able to speak to you.

OPEN THE DOOR

If you never visit your heart, you never get knowledge from the Holy Spirit. When you allow your imagination to open that door, it ushers out visions, dreams, desires, hope, and faith.

Without your imagination working properly, you can go to church every day as the Word keeps pouring in. You may love the Lord, but you aren't helping anyone. You can't even help yourself. You're full of the Word, but you're so heavenly minded, you're of no earthly good. Your heart is filled with faith and with the Word, but you've never learned how to open the door and tap into it.

Occasionally, you have what I call a "faith accident." You have nothing else to think about and your mind wanders. For just a brief moment—you meditate. The instant that door to your heart opens, faith rushes out and you experience mighty blessings. I call it a faith accident because you have no earthly idea that your imagination just kicked in and released the power within. You just shout, "Glory to God!" But you couldn't make it happen again if your life depended on it.

> A man will become what he imagines.

Once again, Proverbs 23:7 says, *"As* [a man] *thinks in his heart, so is he."* Another interpretation of that verse might be, "As a man imagines, so is he." In other words, a man will become what he imagines. He makes an image out of what he sees when he visits his heart. That's the reason Satan works overtime to get your imagination.

And your imagination is hungry.

PAINTING A PICTURE

Your faith is in your heart, not your head. What's in your head is intellect and fact. Those things have no real power. So many people think that faith is believing something with their intellect.

A thousand times, no!

Faith is a spiritual force that resides in your heart. Whenever you go into the realm of the heart, you come out with dreams, visions, hope, and faith.

What your imagination does is paint a picture. Faith sees the picture and goes out to get it. Then you receive it. That's why the Bible says, *"Whatever things you ask when you pray, believe that you receive them, and you will have them"* (Mark 11:24).

Your imagination says to your faith, "Here's a picture. This is what I want." Now faith has something to work with.

We are very, very good at imagining things.

More often than not, we're just not imagining the right things.

Because, although they knew God, they did not glorify Him as God, nor were thankful, but became futile in their thoughts, and their foolish hearts were darkened.

(Romans 1:21)

VAIN IMAGINATIONS

This Scripture relates what happened to born-again Christians who knew God, but remained worldly. *"They knew God, they did not glorify Him as God."* In other words, they didn't do things that glorified God. Their lifestyles didn't give God glory. They did external things for God, but they didn't honor Him on the inside.

"Nor were [they] thankful." The Bible says, *"In everything give thanks"* (1 Thessalonians 5:18). In everything. Can you give thanks for what you did last night? For where you went, for whom you were with, for what you watched? Did your life last night glorify God?

They *"became futile in their thoughts, and their foolish hearts were darkened."* The end result of worldly Christianity is that it becomes vain. One of the definitions of the word *vain* is "empty."

God puts the power to get wealth in your imagination. But if you decide to be worldly or ungodly, God will empty it for you. When your imagination becomes empty, it is ready for all kinds of foolishness. And Satan is ready to accommodate.

FOOLS FOR SATAN

Professing themselves to be wise, they became fools, and changed the glory of the uncorruptible God into an image made like to corruptible man. (Romans 1:22–23 KJV)

God placed an image in their hearts, but they turned around and changed it. How did they change it? First, they made other things a higher priority than God, thereby making their new god their first priority.

When you're a born-again believer, Satan cannot get into your heart. He has no access. His only way to stop you is to tap into your line of communication with God and hijack your imagination. He wants you to use your imagination to lust after things of the world. He desensitizes you to the things you see on television and the movies. These things begin to work on your imagination. Eventually, he assaults you with materialism, pornography, fantasies, and greed—all playing right into the imagination of your heart.

Jesus said that if a man looks at a woman to lust after her (thereby imagining himself with her), then he has already committed adultery. (See Matthew 5:28.) If you are married and you fantasize about yourself with someone other than your spouse, you've committed adultery. Your imagination is not given over to God.

Why do you think the home shopping network shows you the same thing over and over again? Satan is creating an image for you to capture with your imagination. He's trying to find a way into your heart through shopping, through sexual images, through music, or through gossip. You may not say anything, but when you sit there and listen to gossip, you are getting an image created in your imagination.

Many of you are out there drowning, calling for a lifeboat. You need to understand that everything must be brought into obedience to the Word of God. You can cast out demons, but this isn't a demon. It's you. You don't cast it out, you take it down. Like a wrestler, you get it under your foot. Then you capture and take back your own imagination.

You have to arrest your imagination. You must bring *"every thought into captivity to the obedience of Christ"* (2 Corinthians 10:5).

You have to turn the tables on the devil.

Give your imagination to God.

God not only put the idea of spotted rods before Jacob, He has also put a rod before your eyes. It's a rod spotted and stained with the blood of Jesus. He said that whosoever would gaze upon this rod would be changed.

Turn your eyes upon Jesus. Let Him live through you.

Just imagine!

CONFESSION:

Father, I repent of all the ways I've allowed Satan and the world to corrupt my imagination. I want, above all things, to hear Your voice. I want to dream Your dreams and see the visions You have for my life. Give me back the imagination of my childhood innocence. Teach me to tap into my heart through my imagination and loose my faith to bring about Your will in my life. Help me to imagine. Amen.

FAITH KEY #19— RECLAIMING OUR IMAGINATION

There isn't any way to live victoriously as long as Satan has blocked the lines of your communication with God.

Begin with true repentance.

Make a list of things you've done that have changed the image God put inside of you.

Repent for each one and commit to guard your imagination.

Now meditate on how God will communicate to you.

Just imagine!

For though we walk in the flesh, we do not war according to the flesh. For the weapons of our warfare are not carnal but mighty in God for pulling down strongholds, casting down arguments and every high thing that exalts itself against the knowledge of God, bringing every thought into captivity to the obedience of Christ. (2 Corinthians 10:3–5)

Key #20

EMPOWERED TO PROSPER

Continual Sowing into the Purposes of God Makes Your Harvest a Continuous Flow

There is a war over your finances. You need to understand that. Satan knows he lost his legal right to the earth through Jesus' death on the cross. He has no more legal ground to stand on before God, but he is a terrorist and will lie, cheat, steal, and kill in order to control the wealth, thereby controlling the people on earth. But, in addition to his deception, he has another cleverly crafted scheme—he wants to get your money.

If Satan can cause you to sin in the way you handle your finances, he has a legal right to accuse you before God. He is a legalist and will use every loophole to steal what is rightfully yours. If you're going to defeat him, you must understand your legal rights and obligations before God.

In other words, you must understand your contract with God—it's called the New Testament.

Jesus often used the parable of a farmer when explaining how the kingdom of God works. One of the things every farmer understands is that there will be no harvest if no seed is planted. A farmer can't sit back in his recliner and just believe a crop will spring forth if he hasn't prepared the field and planted the seed. Too often, that is exactly what Christians attempt to do.

> When you sow to God's purposes, you will reap a continual harvest.

Likewise, in the kingdom of God, if you need a harvest of finances, it's crucial that you plant your seed (money) into good soil.

> *Let them shout for joy and be glad, who favor my righteous cause; and let them say continually, "Let the LORD be magnified, who has pleasure in the prosperity of His servant."*
>
> (Psalm 35:27)

SOW INTO GOD'S PURPOSES

One of the best places to plant your financial seed is into God's purposes. What are the purposes of God? We find the answer to that in Deuteronomy 8:18,

> *And you shall remember the LORD your God, for it is He who gives you power to get wealth, that He may establish His covenant which He swore to your fathers, as it is this day.*

God will give you the power to get wealth so that He can establish His covenant. In other words, if you plant your finances into seeing that people are born again and established in the kingdom of God, He will grant you the power to get wealth. When you continually sow to God's purposes, you will reap a continual harvest.

148

So how does Satan steal your finances?

He does it the exact same way he did it in the garden of Eden. He whispers to you that God is a liar and that you don't have to obey Him.

"Bring all the tithes into the storehouse, that there may be food in My house, and try Me now in this," says the LORD of hosts, "If I will not open for you the windows of heaven and pour out for you such blessing that there will not be room enough to receive it. And I will rebuke the devourer for your sakes, so that he will not destroy the fruit of your ground, nor shall the vine fail to bear fruit for you in the field," says the LORD of hosts. (Malachi 3:10–11)

One of the first things you can do to become empowered to prosper is to bring all the tithes into the storehouse. Satan really doesn't want you to do that. Even as you read this Scripture he may be whispering to you in much the same way he did to Eve, "You don't have to tithe. That was written to Israelites under the Old Covenant. You have a better covenant and tithing is no longer required. Besides, God understands that things are tight right now. If you want to tithe, you can catch up later."

Every time that happens, you are being tested the same way Adam and Eve were. If you don't think there are real consequences to disobedience, just think about how their sin is still affecting the world today.

THE CAUSE OF THE FALL

God gave Adam everything in the garden except one tree. "Everything is yours except this tree. That's mine."

Satan said, "You won't die! You'll just get as wise as God."

149

It's tempting to believe, isn't it?

You think, *Well, I'll give tithing a try.*

God never told you to try it. He said, "Do it."

God doesn't care what you think about tithing anymore than He cared what Adam thought about leaving that tree alone. The first 10 percent of everything God gives you belongs to Him. Every time someone puts a paycheck or a gift of money in your hand, you're going through the same test Adam went through.

Adam was judged for failing his test.

You and I will be judged for how we respond to God's orders.

It's simple—that money isn't yours.

God made you a steward over it with one condition. The first tenth is His. And I don't mean the first tenth of your net, but your gross. Even Uncle Sam doesn't count your tithe as his own. When you tithe, the government gives you a tax deduction—they don't record it as income.

> The word *blessing* means "empowered to prosper."

The first tenth of your gross belongs to God. If you choose to take what belongs to God, then Satan has a legal right to take what belongs to you.

A LOTTERY MENTALITY

But look what happens when you obey God with the tithe. In Malachi 3:10, God said that if you tithe, He will *"open for you the windows of heaven and pour out for you such blessing that there will not be room enough to receive it."* God isn't trying to get

150

your money; He's trying to get you a blessing. The word *blessing* means "empowered to prosper."

You cannot be empowered to prosper by God unless you tithe.

The sad truth is that most people give the lottery more credit than they give God. The lottery is nothing more than a perversion of Malachi 3:10: "Come buy this lotto ticket, and you can win a jackpot."

People are sowing seed into the world system expecting to be blessed. Do you have any idea what the odds are against your winning? But if you obey God and tithe, you are guaranteed a blessing because God doesn't lie.

The harvest that God wants you to have is a two-part harvest. First, as you give into God's purposes, you will reap a harvest of souls. The second harvest God wants to give you is a harvest of wealth. When you operate in God's kingdom under God's rules, He will make all grace abound to you.

DON'T DISCONNECT

As I mentioned earlier, Satan is a legalist and is constantly attempting to accuse you before God so he can steal your goods. What you have going for you is a covenant contract with God, purchased by the blood of Jesus.

Think of covenant as having a phone conversation. As long as there are two of you talking back and forth, you are connected. If one of you hangs up, or if someone cuts the line, you become disconnected.

Your covenant is your line of communication with God. Obedience in tithing is your "covenant connector." You are under contract with God to obey whatever He tells you to do.

If you disobey, you break your connection. That's exactly what happened to Adam.

Jesus came to earth with one purpose: to restore the covenant connection between God and man.

If you want to be empowered to prosper, keep the line open. Obedience is the key that will unlock the windows of heaven.

CONFESSION:

> Father, forgive me for the times I've muttered and complained about my financial problems when I am the one who opened the door that allowed Satan to steal my goods. Forgive me for disobeying You and disconnecting the "covenant connection" that Jesus died to give to me. Help me be a good steward of all that You place in my hand. Amen.

FAITH KEY #20—
BE EMPOWERED TO PROSPER

Let each one give as he purposes in his heart, not grudgingly or of necessity; for God loves a cheerful giver.
(2 Corinthians 9:7)

The Bible tells us that we are to purpose in our heart what we are going to give. That sounds like a firm decision that defies compromise—no matter the circumstances.

The second condition that God puts on our giving is that we do it cheerfully. When you study the Scripture for yourself and discover all the benefits of the covenant that comes through this divine connection, you'll get excited about giving.

And God is able to make all grace abound toward you,
that you, always having all sufficiency in all things, may
have an abundance for every good work.

(2 Corinthians 9:8)

Key #21

SOW INTO YOUR MAN (OR WOMAN) OF GOD

For the Manifestation of Your Blessing, God Always Looks to Your Man (or Woman) of God

I could write a whole book on how important it is that each of you become rooted and grounded in a local church. One of the reasons is found in Hosea 4:6: *"My people are destroyed for lack of knowledge."* You need to be taught the Word of God and how to apply biblical principles in your life. You need to learn how to live victoriously in every situation.

That will not happen if you disconnect yourself from the church—and the men and women of God who have been appointed as your spiritual leaders.

There is a connection between you and your man or woman of God that most people don't understand. I hazard to guess that this is a vital key that is missing in many Christians' faith lives. To understand this principle, take a look at what God said through the prophet Ezekiel.

154

So I sought for a man among them who would make a wall, and stand in the gap before Me on behalf of the land, that I should not destroy it; but I found no one. (Ezekiel 22:30)

God looked for someone who would stand in the gap and bring a blessing to a people, but He found no one. So God looked in heaven and chose the very best He had to offer. He chose Jesus. He basically said, "I need the Word to become flesh and dwell among them." (See John 1:14.)

This Scripture is very familiar to Christians, but most miss the principle: God is still looking for someone through whom He can bless His people.

Your man or woman of God, your spiritual leader, is your connection to blessing. His or her job is to get you to stop believing with your head and start believing with your heart, because you can have whatever you believe in your heart.

THE KEY TO YOUR MIRACLE

Tithing is a covenant connection between you and God. When you tithe, you are saying to God, "You gave your best for me; now I give my best to You."

Tithing sets the stage for financial blessing; offerings bring forth the manifestation. Offerings are anything that you willingly give over and above the tithe. There are many places to sow your financial seed as offerings before the Lord, but one of the most important, yet overlooked places, is to sow into your man or woman of God.

We see a picture of this principle in the relationship between Elijah and Elisha:

Now Elijah took his mantle, rolled it up, and struck the water; and it was divided this way and that, so that the two of them crossed over on dry ground. And so it was, when they had crossed over, that Elijah said to Elisha, "Ask! What may I do for you, before I am taken away from you?" Elisha said, "Please let a double portion of your spirit be upon me." So he said, "You have asked a hard thing. Nevertheless, if you see me when I am taken from you, it shall be so for you; but if not, it shall not be so." Then it happened, as they continued on and talked, that suddenly a chariot of fire appeared with horses of fire, and separated the two of them; and Elijah went up by a whirlwind into heaven. And Elisha saw it, and he cried out, "My father, my father, the chariot of Israel and its horsemen!" So he saw him no more. And he took hold of his own clothes and tore them into two pieces. He also took up the mantle of Elijah that had fallen from him, and went back and stood by the bank of the Jordan. Then he took the mantle of Elijah that had fallen from him, and struck the water, and said, "Where is the LORD God of Elijah?" And when he also had struck the water, it was divided this way and that; and Elisha crossed over.

(2 Kings 2:8–14)

When the time came for Elisha to be blessed, God took the mantle of Elijah and put it on him. The anointing that Elisha walked in was from his man of God. That principle is just as true for you as it was for him. When Elisha sowed into Elijah's life, he sowed into the anointing of God.

> You should cultivate your giving so that something is ripe all the time.

Think about it from the perspective of the farmer. No farmer would sow all his seed in wheat and have no string beans for fall harvest and no corn in early spring. Each harvest has a season, and so do spiritual things.

You should cultivate your giving so that something is ripe all the time. In doing that, remember that one of the most important places to sow is into your man or woman of God.

How then shall they call on Him in whom they have not believed? And how shall they believe in Him of whom they have not heard? And how shall they hear without a preacher? (Romans 10:14)

DON'T STOP YOUR CROP

A lot of Christians are sowing, but still not seeing the manifestation of their harvest. One thing that will stop your crop is a lack of faith.

This link is found in Hebrews 11:6:

But without faith it is impossible to please Him, for he who comes to God must believe that He is, and that He is a rewarder of those who diligently seek Him.

I want to show you a woman who believed that God would reward her for seeking Him. She understood that her miracle was linked to the mantle of the man or woman of God.

As Jesus and the disciples were going to the rabbi's home, a woman who had been sick for twelve years with internal bleeding came up behind him and touched a tassel of his robe, for she thought, "If I only touch him, I will be healed." Jesus turned around and spoke to her. "Daughter," he said, "all is well! Your faith has healed you." And the woman was well from that moment. (Matthew 9:19–22 TLB)

CONFESSION:

> Father, open my eyes so that I can see the mantle and covenant connection You have placed on my man (or woman) of God. Direct my giving and show me how to sow into his (or her) life and anointing. Thank You for him (or her). Bring all the blessings of the new covenant on him (or her). Give him (or her) fresh revelation from heaven. In Jesus' name I pray. Amen.

FAITH KEY #21—
SOW INTO YOUR MAN (OR WOMAN) OF GOD

The most important decision you make in your Christian walk may be where you are connected in the body of Christ. Many believers choose a church based on how they like the music, what kind of children's programs they offer, whether or not they can find a parking place, or perhaps because they were offended by the leadership of their last church. These are not scriptural reasons for choosing a church and may be dangerous. While there is a passing down of spiritual blessings from your man or woman of God, there can also be transference of the wrong kind of spirits.

There is no way for you to know a person's heart, but God knows.

If you aren't planted in a local church, pray and seek God for His divine direction. When He leads you to the place where you're assigned, don't leave your post. It's a dangerous time to be AWOL in the body of Christ.

Don't be deceived into thinking that your man or woman of God is a televangelist. I preach on television myself and believe that media is a great way to share the gospel, but while

I impart the Word of God into those lives, I am not their man of God. There is no place in the gospel where it says, "How beautiful is the remote control."

Link yourself to the mantle of those God puts in authority over you.

Your miracle is waiting.

And how shall they preach unless they are sent? How beautiful are the feet of those who preach the gospel of peace, who bring glad tidings of good things! (Romans 10:15)

Key #22

YOUR BEST INVESTMENT

When You Give to the Poor,
You Lend to God

"In the United States, stocks fell overnight after the Federal Reserve kept official interest rates at one percent—a forty-five-year low. The stock market weakened in Australia following the negative lead from Wall Street. India is experiencing a bull run, while the Securities and Exchange Board of India asserts that their stock market is undervalued."

T his is the kind of report you hear every day on radio business reports. Most of it flies over the heads of the average Joe.

How do you know how to invest? You won't find the only "sure thing" in life listed on the NASDAQ. It isn't reflected by the Dow Jones Industrial Average.

What is it? A solemn promise by God.

You may already know what God has to say about debt. Romans 13:8 says, *"Owe no one anything except to love one another, for he who loves another has fulfilled the law."*

The Bible also says, *"The rich rules over the poor, and the borrower is servant to the lender"* (Proverbs 22:7).

Owe no one anything except love. The borrower is servant to the lender. Those statements make the Lord's stand on debt pretty clear. Right? Yet in Proverbs, God outlines a situation that will put Him in debt to you:

> *He who has pity on the poor lends to the LORD, and He will pay back what he has given.* (Proverbs 19:17)

Did you get the significance of that promise? If you give to the poor, you have lent to God! That means He is in your debt. By God's own Word, that makes Him a servant to you until He repays the debt. That's one debt that will be paid in full—fast.

> If you give to the poor, you have lent to God!

Isn't it interesting that God says to owe man nothing, but He gives you permission to put Him in debt to you? That makes giving to the poor the safest investment in the world.

POVERTY DEFINED

The definition of *poverty* is "not having what you need to survive." If you don't have enough food, money, clothes, or a place to live, you're in poverty. By that definition, you don't need to give Bill Gates any money. Right?

While it's obvious that Mr. Gates doesn't need your money, there is more than one kind of poverty. Poverty can be natural or spiritual. I don't pretend to know Bill Gates' spiritual condition, but let's assume for the sake of argument that he is not born again. Spiritual poverty occurs when someone doesn't have what they need to survive spiritually, for all of eternity.

So if Bill Gates were not a believer, although he is the wealthiest man in the world, he would be poor in spirit. And you, who have everything you need eternally, are rich.

I believe that God will be indebted to you if you meet the physical needs of those physically poor, and He will be indebted to you if you meet the spiritual needs of those who are poor in spirit.

GOD'S RELIEF PROGRAM

God always warns His people of coming wars, famines, and crises. He speaks through His prophets, but His message is usually not a popular one. That's why many people criticized, and even killed, the prophets.

> *O Jerusalem, Jerusalem, the one who kills the prophets and stones those who are sent to her! How often I wanted to gather your children together, as a hen gathers her chicks under her wings, but you were not willing!*
>
> (Matthew 23:37)

In Acts 11 we see that God sent a prophet to warn the church at Antioch that a time of great lack was coming. It was the kindness of God that warned of this impending disaster.

> *And in these days prophets came from Jerusalem to Antioch. Then one of them, named Agabus, stood up and showed*

by the Spirit that there was going to be a great famine throughout all the world, which also happened in the days of Claudius Caesar. Then the disciples, each according to his ability, determined to send relief to the brethren dwelling in Judea. This they also did, and sent it to the elders by the hands of Barnabas and Saul. (Acts 11:27–30)

The Lord warned His people what would happen so that they could be prepared. They believed what Agabus prophesied and began to prepare. What if Agabus had been wrong? Suppose he had been a false prophet? No big deal. The people would have been okay. But what if he had been right? Then the people would have been in trouble.

> When the church functions correctly, there will be no need.

Notice God's relief plan here. He didn't depend on the Roman government to dole out food. He didn't depend on the Antioch city council to solve the problem.

GOD'S RELIEF PROGRAM WORKS THROUGH HIS CHURCH

The prophet of God declared what would happen. The disciples brought the problem to the elders. The elders spread the word, and the church sent relief to those who had a need. When the church functions correctly, there will be no need.

The reason it doesn't function this way now is because Satan has cleverly separated the church through buildings, denominational divisions, and competition. We have to be wise enough to go back to the Word of God and walk in love.

HOW GOD WILL REPAY

God said that if you give to the poor, He will repay. How will He do that? Where will the money come from?

Give, and it shall be given unto you; good measure, pressed down, and shaken together, and running over, shall men give into your bosom. For with the same measure that ye mete withal it shall be measured to you again. (Luke 6:38 KJV)

The Bible says that when you give, men will give into your bosom. God will take from the wicked and make sure it gets back to you. It will be a transfer of wealth. God will transfer wealth from the wicked to the righteous.

When you give to the poor, you'd better get ready for a promotion on your job. When you give to the poor, get ready to be off unemployment because God is about to open doors for you. When doors start opening for you, you'll be promoted. Your sales commissions will increase.

I have to tell you the truth about giving to the poor. This is insider trading:

You cannot lose.

CONFESSION:

Father, I pray that You open my eyes to the poor around me—those who are poor in finances, as well as those who are poor in spirit. Give me seed to sow into their lives, and I trust You to repay. Amen.

FAITH KEY #22—YOUR BEST INVESTMENT

If you sit down with a financial planner to help you invest for your future, one of the things he'll tell you is to diversify.

In other words, he will not advise you to put all your money in long-term stocks. He might suggest that you invest no more than 10 percent of your portfolio in gold. He might suggest a dependable slow-growing stock for your retirement. He might recommend a riskier investment for those who are younger or getting a late start.

The same is true in the spirit. Tithing opens communication with the best Financial Planner in the universe. All your giving—to the poor, to your man or woman of God, to missions, and to evangelism—are ways of diversifying your seed.

Investing in God's plan is not a risk.

It's an adventure in faith that pays dividends that are out of this world.

Blessed are the poor in spirit, for theirs is the kingdom of heaven. (Matthew 5:3)

Key #23

LEAVE AN INHERITANCE

A Good Man Leaves an Inheritance
to His Children's Children

What we consider a "good" man to be is usually different from God's definition. For instance, Proverbs 13:22 says, *"A good man leaves an inheritance to his children's children."*

This flies in the face of the popular doctrine that to be godly you must be poor. The Bible says you're not a good man unless you leave an inheritance not only to your children, but your grandchildren!

That takes money, folks. The people who think that money is of no consequence to God are going to be surprised on judgment day. Jesus stood at the door of the temple and watched what people put into the offering. I have news for you.

He is still watching.

God is vitally interested, not only in what you do with the tithe, but in how you handle the other 90 percent of the money that comes into your hands. If you're still not sure about this, take a look at this parable that Jesus taught:

A nobleman living in a certain province was called away to the distant capital of the empire to be crowned king of his province. Before he left he called together ten assistants and gave them each $2,000 to invest while he was gone. But some of his people hated him and sent him their declaration of independence, stating that they had rebelled and would not acknowledge him as their king. Upon his return he called in the men to whom he had given the money, to find out what they had done with it, and what their profits were. The first man reported a tremendous gain— ten times as much as the original amount! "Fine!" the king exclaimed. "You are a good man. You have been faithful with the little I entrusted to you, and as your reward, you shall be governor of ten cities." The next man also reported a splendid gain—five times the original amount. "All right!" his master said. "You can be governor over five cities." But the third man brought back only the money he had started with. "I've kept it safe," he said, "because I was afraid (you would demand my profits), for you are a hard man to deal with, taking what isn't yours and even confiscating the crops that others plant." "You vile and wicked slave," the king roared. "Hard, am I? That's exactly how I'll be toward you! If you knew so much about me and how tough I am, then why didn't you deposit the money in the bank so that I could at least get some interest on it?" Then turning to the others standing by he ordered,

> God is interested not only in your tithe but what you do with the other 90 percent of your money.

167

"Take the money away from him and give it to the man who earned the most." "But, sir," they said, "he has enough already!" "Yes," the king replied, "but it is always true that those who have, get more, and those who have little, soon lose even that." (Luke 19:12–26 TLB)

The first thing I want you to notice is that God called the man who made the most profit on his investment a *"good man."* The second thing I want you to notice is the way they handled money determined how—or if—they would rule and reign. The man who increased his money tenfold was told he would rule over ten cities.

THE STOCK MARKET

You may be surprised to know that the stock market is based on God's principles. We know this because it works. If it works, it didn't come from the devil. The devil can't create. All he can do is imitate and pervert. The Bible says that *"every good and perfect gift...comes down from the Father of lights"* (James 1:17).

The world is taking God's principles and using them to gain wealth. You might say they've received a harvest. Most people don't know how to receive, so they go to a stock broker. The broker says, "We have this thing called a mutual fund that will help you diversify your investments. We'll invest a little here and a little there in order to get something back."

The way this works in the world system is they hoard and store up wealth for themselves. At least, they think they are.

Remember the verse we started with? Proverbs 13:22 says, *"A good man leaves an inheritance for his children's children."* I just quoted the first half of that Scripture. Now let's look at it in its

168

entirety, *"A good man leaves an inheritance to his children's chil- dren, but the wealth of the sinner is stored up for the righteous."*

The wealth of the sinner is stored up for the righteous!

The *Amplified Bible* says,

A good man leaves an inheritance [of moral stability and goodness] to his children's children, and the wealth of the sinner [finds its way eventually] into the hands of the righ- teous, for whom it was laid up.

In a way, God uses the wicked as His own personal sav- ings account. The wicked think the money is theirs. They work hard to lay up wealth, but it's in God's account. Satan doesn't own anything because the earth, and everything in it, belongs to someone else.

The earth is the Lord's, and all its fullness, the world and those who dwell therein. For He has founded it upon the seas, and established it upon the waters. (Psalm 24:1–2)

GOD'S MONEY MARKET

The Lord can certainly count. He has numbered all the hairs on your head, and He has numbered all the accounts of the wicked. God's saying, "Go ahead and store it up. I know your account number. I've got your number, and that account is stored up for the just."

God is not mocked. He sent the money down, and He will eventually get it into the hands of the just. That means we need to know and live out God's definition of the "just."

If you are born again, you are declared just and righteous before God. If you merely join a church, or pretend to be a Christian, that does not mean anything is laid up for you. God knows your heart. You have to get it right, because although you might fool some people, you will not fool the Lord.

Some of you are standing up and commanding that money to come to you now. I have news for you. It's not in your account to command. You have to do what is right, and you have to be financially responsible to get it.

> In God's financial situation, God pays back according to His riches in glory.

There is no need for you to confess that it's coming because it isn't. Why?

If God released that money to you now, the devil would get it in a heartbeat.

Far too many believers simply aren't wise about their finances. If you're going to get in on the transfer of wealth, you're going to have to wise up.

The first step is tithing.

The second step is knowing where to sow your seeds of offering. I've already suggested that you sow into your man or woman of God and into the poor.

One who increases his possessions by usury and extortion gathers it for him who will pity the poor. (Proverbs 28:8)

The Living Bible translates the same passage this way:

Income from exploiting the poor will end up in the hands of someone who pities them.

GOD'S FINANCIAL SYSTEM

When you glimpse God's financial system, you'll see that God pays back according to His riches in glory. Let me give you an example.

One day you run an errand for your boss and deliver a package to a business across the street from a park. It's a lovely spring day and children are playing on swings, on slides, and tossing a ball, as their parents or caretakers watch from nearby benches. As you step off the sidewalk to where your car is parked, a large red ball rolls into the street. Looking up from the lock on your car door, you see a little girl dash into the street after the ball. A truck is headed straight for her, and no one else is close enough to help.

Without thinking, you throw yourself at the child, grab her, and roll to safety, only inches from the tires of the oncoming truck. Her babysitter runs up in hysterics and insists on taking down your name.

Still shaken, you get in your car and drive back to work.

When the child's father gets home that day and hears how you saved his child, he decides to reward you. You had no idea that the little girl was Bill Gates' daughter.

When Bill Gates, the richest man in the world, rewards you, you know you've been rewarded. He will not send a loaf of banana bread and a card. No amount of money in the world could give him what you just saved—the life of his child. Bill Gates will reward you by Bill Gates' standards.

God is much richer than Bill Gates. When you rescue His children, He will reward you according to His standards. The wealth of the wicked will be transferred into your accounts.

Your grandchildren will buy out Bill Gates.

CONFESSION:

Father, I ask that You teach me how Your financial system works. I ask that You give me a kingdom mentality and financial wisdom. Teach me how to invest, both spiritually and financially, to leave an inheritance for my children and grandchildren. Forgive me for being unwise with the money You put into my hand. Make me like the wise servant who brings back a profit to You. I ask this in Jesus' name. Amen.

FAITH KEY #23—LEAVE AN INHERITANCE

As you begin a new life of financial wisdom, seek counsel from godly men and women whom the Lord has given an anointing for wealth. Don't be too prideful to admit that you've made mistakes and need to learn a new way to handle finances.

Whatever you do, don't make the mistake of falling into "get-rich-quick" schemes. God builds everything in His kingdom line upon line, and precept upon precept. He does not want you to miss the wisdom that comes through the diligence of planning, budgeting, saving, and investing money.

Proverbs 28:22 says, *"Trying to get rich quick is evil and leads to poverty"* (TLB).

If you are a faithful tither, ask God for wisdom and the anointing to handle the other 90 percent. Above all, obey Him or, like the children of Israel, you'll just wander around the desert of lack and debt for years and years.

The man who wants to do right will get a rich reward. But the man who wants to get rich quick will quickly fail.
(Proverbs 28:20 TLB)

Key #24

GET A GRIP ON GRACE

The Church Is in Bondage
Because We Do Not Understand Grace

I n the Old Testament, the word *grace* was really the Hebrew word for "graciousness." That word, *checed*, means "to show undeserved favor, mercy, and pity upon someone." We find an example of that in 2 Samuel 9.

David was king of Israel, and both King Saul and his son, Jonathan, were dead. David discovered that Jonathan's son, Mephibosheth, was still alive, although lame in both feet.

So King David sent for Mephibosheth, who arrived in great fear and greeted the king in deep humility, bowing low before him. But David said,

> *Do not fear, for I will surely show you kindness for Jonathan your father's sake, and will restore to you all the land of Saul your grandfather; and you shall eat bread at my table continually.* (2 Samuel 9:7)

Mephibosheth fell to the ground before the king and asked, *"What is your servant, that you should look upon such a dead dog as I?"* (2 Samuel 9:8).

Then the king summoned Saul's servant, Ziba, and told him,

I have given to your master's son all that belonged to Saul and to all his house. You therefore, and your sons and your servants, shall work the land for him, and you shall bring in the harvest, that your master's son may have food to eat. But Mephibosheth your master's son shall eat bread at my table always. (verses 9–10)

Ziba agreed, and the king declared,

"As for Mephibosheth," said the king, "he shall eat at my table like one of the king's sons." (verse 11)

What David did for Mephibosheth is a perfect picture of Old Testament grace. Although Mephibosheth had done nothing to deserve it, David was gracious to him, showering him with pity and mercy. Until Jesus came, what could mankind hope for except pity and mercy?

A DANGEROUS DECEPTION

One of the most dangerous deceptions ever perpetrated against the church happened when people just accepted that the Old Testament definition of grace did not change with Jesus.

And the Word became flesh and dwelt among us, and we beheld His glory, the glory as of the only begotten of the Father, full of grace and truth. (John 1:14)

For years we assumed that Jesus was full of *checed* ("to show undeserved favor, mercy, and pity upon someone.")

We assumed wrong, and Satan perpetrated the lie.

The church has been in bondage for two thousand years simply because we have not understood New Testament grace. During that time, we've known of the Old Testament *grace*—"God's unmerited favor"—meaning that we, like Mephibosheth, are merely "dead dogs" to whom God extended undeserved mercy.

The reason God gave us His mercy was that we were sinners. But if grace is mercy, the words should be interchangeable. In Romans 1:7, Paul says,

To all who are in Rome, beloved of God, called to be saints: Grace to you and peace from God our Father and the Lord Jesus Christ.

In almost every letter Paul wrote to the churches, he said, *"Grace be unto you."* If we use the Old Testament definition of *grace*, then he is advising the saints, in effect, "Keep on sinning, and I'll ask God to give you more of that undeserved mercy and favor." However, Paul also teaches that we are not to see ourselves as "dead dogs" at the feet of God.

> God's empowering presence enables you to be who He called you to be.

Be diligent to present yourself approved to God, a worker who does not need to be ashamed, rightly dividing the word of truth. (2 Timothy 2:15)

GOD'S EMPOWERING PRESENCE

The reason it doesn't make sense is because we've pulled the Old Testament definition of *grace* into the New Covenant.

175

That's the reason Satan has backed up his truck and is loading up all our blessings and carrying them away.

Don't get me wrong, God did extend His mercy to us. In His gracious kindness, Jesus died on the cross for us. His mercy gave us something we didn't deserve. He gave us heaven when we deserved hell. He took us out of darkness and gave us light. He healed us when we deserved sickness and death.

But now, according to Romans 8:1–2,

There is therefore now no condemnation to those who are in Christ Jesus, who do not walk according to the flesh, but according to the Spirit. For the law of the Spirit of life in Christ Jesus has made me free from the law of sin and death.

We've been delivered from the law of sin and death, and there is no condemnation for those who are in Christ Jesus. *The Amplified Bible* says that there is *"no adjudging guilty of wrong."* We are no longer guilty. We've been judged and the verdict is "Innocent!" Why would we need the undeserved favor and mercy of God? The answer is simple. We don't.

So what is the New Testament definition of *grace*? It is God's empowering presence that enables you to be who God called you to be and to do what He called you to do.

Grace isn't mercy.

Grace is the power of God moving in your circumstances.

Grace is a key to personal and professional success.

CONFESSION:

Father, help me to not only understand grace, but to access it in order to become all that You have called me to be. Amen.

FAITH KEY #24—GET A GRIP ON GRACE

By misunderstanding grace, we've not only missed out on how to access the great power that God has released to us for successful living, but we've also been duped into thinking that we're pitiful. We still have a mind-set that we're nothing but "an old sinner saved by grace."

Those lies are negative strongholds in our thinking.

We were pitiful until Jesus made us righteous.

We were old sinners, but now we're new creations—saints of God.

These may seem like no more than semantics, but they are religious strongholds that must be destroyed so that we can step into our destiny.

It's no wonder pity parties don't move God.

How can God pity us when He has given us His best?

When He looks at you, He sees Jesus.

But as many as received Him, to them He gave the right to become children of God, to those who believe in His name: who were born, not of blood, nor of the will of the flesh, nor of the will of man, but of God. (John 1:12–13)

Key #25

BOLDLY APPROACH THE THRONE OF GOD

We Have Been Approaching the Throne of God for Mercy When We Need Grace

The devil does not want you to get a revelation of grace. The world doesn't want you to figure it out. Once you find out what grace is all about, you're going to start marching. When you start marching, you're going to take back everything the devil has stolen from you. There's a mighty army getting ready to rise up in this land by the grace of God.

You may have the worst sales record of any salesman in the country, but when you realize that the empowering presence of God is in your life, that is going to change. You'll look in the mirror each morning and think, *If God is with me, who can stand against me? If God is on my side, whom shall I fear?*

When you understand this revelation, your faith will start operating all the time. It will revolutionize your life.

*Seeing then that we have a great High Priest who has passed through the heavens, Jesus the Son of God, let us hold fast our confession. For we do not have a High Priest who cannot sympathize with our weaknesses, but was in all points tempted as we are, yet without sin. **Let us therefore come boldly to the throne of grace,** that we may obtain mercy and find grace to help in time of need.*

(Hebrews 4:14–16, emphasis added)

TAKE YOUR WEAKNESS TO THE THRONE

The Bible tells us to come boldly and confidently to the throne of grace. You're not supposed to slink up there like a dog with its tail between its legs, feeling undeserving.

Take your weakness boldly to the throne of God, because that's where His empowering presence abides. At the throne of grace you will find two things: mercy and grace in your time of need.

This passage of Scripture tells us to take our weakness to the throne. You cannot tap into God's grace—His power—unless you acknowledge that you need His help. That empowering presence is given to help you do what God has called you to do.

> You cannot tap into God's grace unless you acknowledge that you need His help.

A lot of Christians are missing it because they want God to do the job for them. "Lord, help me! Lord, deliver me! Lord, I've been calling for months." That's not the way grace works. God gives grace to empower you so the two of you (you and God) can do what needs to be done.

THORN IN THE FLESH

"But Pastor McLean, I know that Scripture. I always go boldly to the throne. Why is nothing changing?"

Christians approach the throne room all the time, but most have no idea what to look for from God. They're not looking for God's empowering presence—His grace.

Don't feel bad. Paul had the same problem.

In 2 Corinthians 12, Paul described an incredible experience he had when God allowed him to visit heaven. He talked about himself in the third person—as if it were somebody else. In this vision, he was shown incredible things and he heard incredible words that was not allowed to utter. You can see Paul's struggle with his own pride.

> *Of such a one I will boast; yet of myself I will not boast, except in my infirmities. For though I might desire to boast, I will not be a fool; for I will speak the truth. But I refrain, lest anyone should think of me above what he sees me to be or hears from me. And lest I should be exalted above measure by the abundance of the revelations, a thorn in the flesh was given to me, a messenger of Satan to buffet me, lest I be exalted above measure. Concerning this thing I pleaded with the Lord three times that it might depart from me.*
>
> (2 Corinthians 12:5–8)

The word *buffet* means "to hit repeatedly." Satan will attempt to do the same thing to you as he did to Paul. He will come at you repeatedly to hinder you from walking out your revelation from God. That's why you can expect him to try to hinder you from understanding the revelation of grace.

THE NUMBER OF GRACE

The Bible says that Paul came before the throne of grace three times. Why three times? First, three is the number of God's grace. When God came into your life, He came through grace—the Father, Son and Holy Spirit. He imparted the kingdom of God to you in threes—righteousness, peace, and joy in the Holy Spirit. How did Jesus save you? Through the death, burial, and resurrection. God always pours out His grace in threes.

Paul went before God three times. The first two times he heard no response. He went back to plead with God a third time when God answered him, saying, *"My grace is sufficient for you"* (2 Corinthians 12:9).

Perhaps Paul didn't hear anything the first two times because he went looking for mercy. Mercy is easy to obtain. All you have to do is reach out and take it. Forty-one times the Bible says, *"God's mercy endures forever."* Scripture also says that His mercies are renewed each morning. (See Lamentations 3:23.)

Perhaps the problem was the fact that Paul still thought of grace as he knew it under the Old Covenant. He didn't need mercy. He was in need of God's empowering presence to enable him to deal with that demon.

To paraphrase 2 Corinthians 12:9 above: "My empowering presence is all you need. It will enable you to be all that I called you to be, and do all that I've called you to do."

God didn't tell Paul to crawl and beg for mercy. He was saying, in effect, "Don't you know that My grace—My empowering presence—is enough to overcome any danger or battle you face? I know you're wrestling with this, but My empowering presence will strengthen you. My presence is the perfect match to your weakness."

Paul came looking for mercy but found grace. Afterward, Paul pledged not to brag about his revelation, but in his weakness, which allowed God's grace to provide the muscle.

Therefore I take pleasure in infirmities, in reproaches, in needs, in persecutions, in distresses, for Christ's sake. For when I am weak, then I am strong.

(2 Corinthians 12:10)

A revelation of grace will take away the shame and reproach many of you feel. You may be ashamed of your past. You may be ashamed of what you cannot do. When you discover what Paul discovered, you'll never be ashamed again.

The great grace of God—His empowering presence—is activated in your weakness.

Do what Paul did.

Boldly approach the throne of grace.

CONFESSION:

Father, forgive me for murmuring against You when I've been in a battle and approached Your throne for mercy when what I needed was Your grace. Thank you for Your empowering presence in the midst of my weakness. I confess that I am weak and You are strong. I cannot accomplish what You've called me to do without Your empowering presence. Thank You for being all that I need. Amen.

FAITH KEY #25—
BOLDLY APPROACH THE THRONE OF GOD

I have never been caught up into heaven the way Paul was, but I once knew a man (me) whose tongue was tied and couldn't speak. I knew a man who was hurt, depressed, and discouraged. He carried emotional pain and scars every day of his life. I once knew a man who failed at everything he tried to do. His best was never enough.

He was told, "You can't preach because you can't talk."

He was told, "You'll never be a success in the business world because of the color of your skin."

Those people were right about that man.

I once knew him.

But I hardly remember him today.

Today I am able to boast in my weakness because, in my desperation, I went boldly before the throne of God and found help in time of trouble.

God's grace was sufficient for me.

His empowering presence is sufficient for you.

This is the word of the Lord to Zerubbabel:

"Not by might nor by power, but by My Spirit," says the LORD of hosts. "Who are you, O great mountain? Before Zerubbabel you shall become a plain! And he shall bring forth the capstone with shouts of 'Grace, grace to it!'"

(Zechariah 4:6–7)

Key #26

EMPOWERED BY HIS PRESENCE

Jesus Needed the Empowering Presence of God
in His Life to Do What He Was Called to Do

The Greek word for *grace* is *charis,* which means "a spiritual act of divine influence upon the heart of man that is reflected in his life." From that definition I wrote my own definition for *grace*: "the empowering presence of God, which enables you to be who He called you to be and to do what He called you to do."

Do you realize now that "unmerited favor" was an Old Testament definition that does not fit Jesus?

In light of the new definition, let's look at John 1:14 again with my definition of *grace* inserted:

And the Word was made flesh, and dwelt among us, and we beheld his glory, the glory as of the only begotten of the Father, full of [the empowering presence of God, which enabled Him to be what He was created to be and to do what He was called to do] *and truth.*

You have to understand that when Jesus left heaven, He needed grace. He stripped Himself of his glory and came to earth in the form of a man. This grace—the empowering presence of God in a man—was something new.

Now let's take a fresh look at Luke 2:40:

And the Child grew and became strong in spirit, filled with wisdom; and the grace [empowering presence] *of God was upon Him.*

The reason Jesus was successful in His earthly ministry wasn't because He was God. It was because of God's empowering presence. Now you understand what Paul was talking about over and over in his letters to the churches when he said, *"Grace be upon you!"* He was saying, "May the empowering presence of God be upon you as it was upon Jesus!"

NO MORE PITY PARTIES

Peter went even further than Paul. He said, *"May grace...be multiplied to you"* (1 Peter 1:2; 2 Peter 1:2 RSV). In other words, "May the empowering presence of God, which enables you to do and be all that He has called you to do, be multiplied to you!"

And of His fullness we have all received, and grace for grace. (John 1:16)

For years Christians have filled the altars of God wailing for pity because they thought it was grace.

"Lord, I don't have enough money."

"My family is going to starve!"

"Lord, my husband left, and I'm destitute!"

You don't have to beg God to pity you anymore. All you have to do is ask for more grace—more of His empowering presence. You are a believer, not a doubter, because you know that God's empowering presence will strengthen you to conquer every problem that comes your way.

There is one example in the Old Testament where grace was accompanied with this New Testament-kind of power:

> *This is the word of the Lord to Zerubbabel: "Not by might nor by power, but by My Spirit," says the LORD of hosts. "Who are you, O great mountain? Before Zerubbabel you shall become a plain! And he shall bring forth the capstone with shouts of 'Grace, grace to it!'"* (Zechariah 4:6–7)

All Zerubbabel had to do was cry "Grace!" and God said that mountains would fall down flat. In light of that, perhaps now we understand what Jesus meant in Matthew 17:18–20:

> *And Jesus rebuked the demon, and he came out of him; and the child was cured from that very hour. Then the disciples came to Jesus privately and said, "Why could we not cast him out?" So Jesus said to them, "Because of your unbelief; for assuredly, I say to you, if you have faith as a mustard seed, you will say to this mountain, 'Move from here to there,' and it will move; and nothing will be impossible for you."*

GRACE WORKS BY FAITH

When you open your mouth and speak to the mountain, what comes out? If you truly believe what you are saying, grace will come out, because grace works by faith.

If grace was mercy, Jesus would have to go back to the cross continually to pay for the sins of the world. But He doesn't ever have to go back to the cross because He brought a whole transformation of grace.

You need two things to receive the kingdom of God: one is grace, and the other is righteousness.

> *For if by one man's offence death reigned by one; much more they* [believers] *which receive abundance of* [God's empowering presence in their lives, enabling them to be what He created them to be and to do what He called them to do] *and the gift of righteousness shall reign.*
>
> (Romans 5:17 KJV)

WHAT THE DEVIL DOESN'T WANT YOU TO KNOW

How will you reign? You'll reign through the empowering presence of God. All that grace is being poured out on you. It's the same power that raised Jesus from the dead!

Are you beginning to see why the devil is afraid? Do you see why he doesn't want you to understand this? Why you feel like your mind is going through convulsions? The devil does not want this to take root in your heart because, if it does, it's all over for him. He'll have another Jesus on his hands. Trust me, he's whining, "I don't want to face that guy again." He's afraid that Ephesians 1:19–21 is about to come alive in you:

> *And what is the exceeding greatness of His power toward us who believe, according to the working of His mighty power which He worked in Christ when He raised Him from the dead and seated Him at His right hand in the heavenly places, far above all principality and power and might and*

187

dominion, and every name that is named, not only in this age but also in that which is to come.

GRACE AND GLORY

Through His grace, God is bestowing power on you that is above all principalities, all demons, all evil spirits, all sickness, all disease, and everything that is named. What is the exceeding greatness of His power to those of us who believe?

It's the same power that raised Jesus from the dead: God's empowering presence is the manifestation of His glory.

That means when, by faith, Moses held the rod over the Red Sea, God Himself came down and parted it. When, by faith, the children of Israel marched around Jericho seven times, God manifested His presence and brought the walls down.

> God's empowering presence is the manifestation of His glory.

Through Jesus, God is offering that same exceedingly great power to you.

People are running from church to church looking for the glory of God. "We need Your glory!" What they're asking for is available through God's grace—His empowering presence. There is a measure of that operating today, but somebody has to pray. Somebody has to preach. Somebody has to play music. People have to sing and worship the Lord. It is through praise and worship that we are ushered into His presence.

When you've been in God's presence and grace spills over onto you, people will know it. "I know that boy. That's Joe's kid. He's never been any good. What happened to him? That must be God!"

Believers or not, they will give God the glory. "Praise God, that boy is off drugs!" You're a worthy representative of God's grace when people see your life and give Him glory.

The grace of God is yours.

Bask in His empowering presence.

CONFESSION:

Father, thank You for granting me access to Your great glory and grace. Teach me to enter Your presence and find grace to meet all my needs. May the world see Your empowering presence at work in my life and give You all the glory. May this revelation be rooted deep within my heart and be reflected in my life. Amen.

FAITH KEY #26—
EMPOWERED BY HIS PRESENCE

I'm going to be perfectly honest with you. If the only time you enter God's presence is in the sanctuary during corporate worship, you'll have a hard time living in the grace of God.

God's grace is His empowering presence.

If you are going to tap into that grace, you have to learn how to enter His presence, not just in corporate worship, but also at home when your child is burning with fever. The more intimate you become with God, the more confident you'll be to cry "Grace!" over your checkbook, your marriage, or your teenagers who have turned from Him.

Worship God on your bed each morning. Give praise to Him in your car on the way to work. Sing to Him, clap for joy, and when you face a mountain of obstacles, shout "Grace!"

Make a joyful shout to the LORD, all you lands! Serve the LORD with gladness; come before His presence with singing. Know that the LORD, He is God; it is He who has made us, and not we ourselves; we are His people and the sheep of His pasture. Enter into His gates with thanksgiving, and into His courts with praise. Be thankful to Him, and bless His name. For the LORD is good; His mercy is everlasting, and His truth endures to all generations.

(Psalm 100:1–5)

Key #27

GET JESUS IN YOUR BOAT

Jesus Stood Up in the Boat and Said, "Peace, Be Still!"

The water lapped lazily against the wooden boat that Jesus used as a platform from which to preach. Crowds covered the hillside, drinking in His words like a famished people dying of thirst. He taught them through stories of everyday life that they understood.

"A farmer sowed his field..." (Mark 4:26 TLB).

Later, as evening fell, He sent the crowd on their way and told His disciples to take Him to the other side of the lake. The men shoved the boat off from shore and began rowing while Jesus, exhausted from preaching all day, lay in the back of the boat and went to sleep.

Storm clouds gathered, and the wind beat viciously against the boat. Massive waves washed over the side as the men bailed water furiously. Still, Jesus slept.

The boat groaned and creaked, tipping to one side as it began to sink.

And they awoke Him and said to Him, "Teacher, do You not care that we are perishing?" (Mark 4:38)

Jesus rose, stretched, looked at the wind and sea, and uttered, *"Peace, be still!"* (verse 39). Immediately, the wind ceased and the waves calmed. Jesus shook His head and asked them, *"Why are you so fearful? How is it that you have no faith?"* (verse 40).

Have you ever wondered why the winds and waves obeyed? Did they understand that He was the Messiah, a fact that His disciples hadn't yet grasped?

> Speak in faith. Grace will come out, and God will do the rest.

I don't think so. I think the wind and waves responded to grace. Jesus' faith-filled words released the empowering presence of God.

And they were filled with awe and said among themselves, "Who is this man, that even the winds and seas obey him?" (verse 41 TLB)

WHEN GOD SHOWS UP, STUFF HAPPENS

How would you like to have Jesus show up when you're in a boatload of trouble? He will, but you'll have to operate the same way He did. You have to speak faith-filled words. When you speak to the sea, it must obey you. When you speak to your finances, they must obey you. When you speak grace over your marriage, God's empowering presence will show up.

The key thing you have to realize is that it will not be by

your ability. All you have to do is open your mouth and speak in faith. Grace will come out, and God will do the rest.

In order to learn how to activate the grace of God in your life, it's important to dismantle religious thinking. This is a big misconception:

The Holy Spirit is not the power of God.

There, I said it.

Keep breathing, and stay with me for a moment.

The Holy Spirit is not the power of God.

The Holy Spirit IS God.

There's a vast difference. How can your relegate God to only one facet of Himself—His power? You're relegating God to no more than force.

Use your common sense. If I was to pick up a book and hold it in the air, would you call that act me? Of course not, because you know that I'm a lot of things in addition to the power I possess to lift a book. Yet we've relegated the Holy Spirit to just power.

The Holy Spirit IS God.

One thing the Holy Spirit DOES is dispense power.

The reason He dispenses power is because you and I cannot be trusted with it. We don't know what to do with God's power, and we don't know how to use it. Knowing us, we would probably use it selfishly. So, it's a good thing the Bible also calls the Holy Spirit our Helper.

Why? Because we're always needing help!

Grace has been given to you by God. It's with you all the time. When you release faith-filled words, the Holy Spirit helps by manifesting His presence.

Partners in Power

God has given you grace so that you can partake of His power. The word *partake* means "to share in or partner with." Grace—God's empowering presence—allows you to partner with God's power.

The power of God brings peace, *shalom* in Hebrew, which means "whole, set free, delivered, and saved." Another great translation of the word *shalom* is "nothing broken, nothing missing." If you check your life and find that your marriage

> God has given you grace so that you can partake of His power.

isn't broken, none of your children are missing, and you have your health and money—you have peace. But the only way to get that peace is through God's power.

You can be a millionaire and still have your life broken into shards and find your peace missing. You can buy a lot of things trying to fill the void that exists when you don't have the peace of God.

When you have peace in your life, it means that Jesus is in your boat. Just like He did during the storm on the Sea of Galilee, He has spoken, *"Peace! Be still."*

If you don't have peace in every area of your life, and there are storms on the horizon, how do you get Jesus in your boat?

Speak to the storms, and grace—God's empowering presence—will do the rest.

Confession:

Father, I need Jesus in my boat! Teach me to speak to the storms in my life and release the grace of God—

Your empowering presence—to calm every storm. Amen.

FAITH KEY #27—GET JESUS IN YOUR BOAT

Suppose you go to the market and see someone shopping in the same aisle. You have no way of knowing whether that person is desperately sick or if he or she has been seeking God for a miracle. As you pass that person, the Holy Spirit inside of you goes on red alert.

"Go heal that person!"

"Lord, is that You?"

"Go heal that person!"

"I can't heal anyone!"

"Go lay hands on that person and pray."

"What if I do and nothing happens?"

"Just do it."

"I just can't."

"Just do it. My grace is sufficient."

You awkwardly ask the person if you can pray.

The person leaps at the suggestion. You speak faith-filled words of healing. The person thanks you, and you go back to your shopping.

As you walk away, the empowering presence of God wraps itself around that person like a cocoon, penetrating every cell in every tissue of his or her body. Even the soul is washed in the power of God. The same grace that raised Jesus from the dead has healed this person's mortal body. Church has broken out in the produce aisle of the supermarket!

That's grace. Jesus is now in that person's boat.

Not by might, nor by power.

It's by the Spirit of God.

Grace to you and peace from God the Father and our Lord Jesus Christ. (Galatians 1:3)

Key #28

THE THIRD DIMENSION

The Relationship between You and God
Is Called Grace

As I stated before, grace always falls in threes, and there are three different dimensions of grace. The first dimension is the role of the Holy Spirit who helps you by dispensing power into your life. That's why the Holy Spirit is called the Helper. When you are angry, He says, "Let Me give you a little of My power—it's called 'temperance.'" This dimension involves the fruit of the Spirit.

The second dimension of grace is when the Holy Spirit releases the anointing to you. He anoints you with grace to do whatever God wants done. So the Holy Spirit is also the Anointer. This dimension involves the gifts of the Spirit.

The third dimension of grace is the place where everyone wants to live. It is derived from the Greek word *dunato*. It means "able" and refers to God's ability to show Himself powerful. In the third dimension, the Holy Spirit helps by revealing

Himself as the Reviver. This dimension involves God's glory and revival.

THE SPIRIT OF ADOPTION

> *But as many as received Him, to them He gave the right to become children of God, to those who believe in His name.*
>
> (John 1:12)

In this Scripture, John said that God gives power for you to become something. That's interesting to me because the world is always trying to get you to become something, too.

> God gives power for you to become something.

The world tries to get you to become a cheat or a liar. The world wants you to become fearful and depressed. More than anything, the world wants you to become poor.

According to this passage, for *"as many as received Him"* God wants to give the power to become something. What does He want you to become?

The power to become sons and daughters of God.

That's better than being a poor kid adopted into Bill Gates' family.

This is amazing grace.

All you need to do is take your rightful place in the family.

The incredible thing about this grace is that you can mess up, trip out, and live in a pig pen, but if you repent and return to the house, the grace of God will give you back what is rightfully yours.

Bow or Burn

The third chapter of Daniel tells the story of three Hebrew men, Shadrach, Meshach, and Abednego, who lived in Babylonian captivity. These guys were promoted so much that a lot of folks were jealous, and some of them set a trap. The king built an image of gold in his honor and said, in effect, "I want everyone to bow down and worship my image whenever the music is played. Anyone who doesn't bow and worship will be thrown into the fire."

The three men of God refused to bow because they understood that God's presence was with them. The king was furious and summoned them for questioning.

"Is it true, O Shadrach, Meshach, and Abednego," he demanded, "that you are refusing to serve my gods or to worship the gold statue I set up? I'll give you one more chance. When the music plays, if you fall down and worship the statue, all will be well. But if you refuse, you will be thrown into a flaming furnace within the hour. And what god can deliver you out of my hands then?" Shadrach, Meshach, and Abednego replied, "O Nebuchadnezzar, we are not worried about what will happen to us. If we are thrown into the flaming furnace, our God is able [donato] to deliver us; and he will deliver us out of your hand, Your Majesty." (Daniel 3:14–17 TLB)

Be Patient

Some of you need to get a grip on this revelation and reply like Shadrach, Meshach, and Abednego.

"You may lay me off, but I'm going to survive. Why?"

"My God is able!"

199

"You may be trying to destroy my family, but my marriage will survive. Why?"

"My God is able!"

"I may not have enough money to pay my bills, but I'm not going under! Why?"

"My God is able!"

The king ordered the fire to be stoked up even hotter. It was so hot that the men who shoved Shadrach, Meshach, and Abednego into the fire died themselves. In God's time, He will deal with the people trying to destroy you, so pray for them.

The king looked into the fire pit.

"Look!" he answered, "I see four men loose, walking in the midst of the fire; and they are not hurt, and the form of the fourth is like the Son of God." (Daniel 3:25)

Notice that the empowering presence of God didn't show up until Shadrach, Meshach, and Abednego were in the flames. That's the reason that you will need patience.

What did the fourth man do? Nothing. He just showed up. Shadrach, Meshach, and Abednego could not burn because of His presence. The empowering presence of God showed up on the scene. It just showed up and everything changed.

I have news for you: if you won't bow, you won't burn.

And God is able to make all grace abound toward you; that ye, always having all sufficiency in all things, may abound to every good work. (2 Corinthians 9:8 KJV)

Confession:

Father, thank You for the grace that kept Shadrach, Meshach, and Abednego from burning in the fire.

Help me see the times that I lost patience and lost faith before Your power arrived on the scene. I pray that Your grace will keep me from bowing before anything the devil sends my way. In Jesus' name I pray. Amen.

I'm not going under

FAITH KEY #28—THE THIRD DIMENSION

There's something about grace that I want you to understand. You need to know not only that it is your inheritance as a son or daughter of God, but you also need to know where it originated.

Everything in every dimension of grace came from Jesus. The anointing started with Jesus. The power came from Jesus. The fruit originated from Jesus. The gifts came from Jesus.

Jesus came to earth full of grace. That's where it all started.

If you have accepted Jesus into your life and made Him your Lord and Master, then you are a joint-heir with Him. That means everything that Jesus has is now your inheritance.

Grace—in all three dimensions—is at your disposal every moment of every hour of every day.

Live in His empowering presence.

For the law was given by Moses, but grace and truth came by Jesus Christ.   (John 1:17 KJV)

Key #29

DON'T FRUSTRATE THE GRACE

Grace Has Not Worked in Our Lives
Because We Have Not Allowed It to Work

The God of the universe split the atoms of His own being and brought Himself to earth in the form of a man. That's love. He has granted us His grace. He has offered us His empowering presence. There is nothing that He has withheld from us.

So why are so many of us living far below our position in the God Class?

It's because we're frustrating the grace of God.

God is able to make all grace abound to us, but we aren't allowing it.

To be perfectly honest—we aren't obedient.

There is no need to hide from the truth because we cannot hide from God. It's not like He doesn't already know this.

Obedience is settling your heart on a no-compromise stand with God. God isn't like your mother or your father. He isn't like your favorite grade school teacher. He isn't even like your kind old college professor.

He was there before creation.

He hung the sun, moon, and stars in their places.

He told the tide how far it could travel.

He set the boundaries of the seas and called into being all that is seen.

With God, certain issues are non-negotiable. Yet too many believers are still trying to work out a deal, and in doing so, they find themselves tripping over the same things.

Then the Lord answered Job from the whirlwind: "Why are you using your ignorance to deny my providence? Now get ready to fight, for I am going to demand some answers from you, and you must reply. Where were you when I laid the foundations of the earth? Tell me, if you know so much. Do you know how its dimensions were determined, and who did the surveying? What supports its foundations, and who laid its cornerstone as the morning stars sang together and all the angels shouted for joy? Who decreed the boundaries of the seas when they gushed from the depths? Who clothed them with clouds and thick darkness and barred them by limiting their shores, and said, 'Thus far and no farther shall you come, and here shall your proud waves stop!'? Have you ever once commanded the morning to appear and caused the dawn to rise in the east? Have you ever told the daylight to spread to the ends of the earth, to end the night's wickedness? Have you ever robed the dawn in red, and disturbed the haunts of wicked men, and stopped the arm raised to strike? Have you explored the springs from which the seas come, or walked in the sources of their depths? Has the location of the gates of Death been revealed to you? Do you realize the extent of the earth? Tell me about it if you know! Where does the light come from, and how do you get there? Or tell me about the darkness. Where does it come from? Can you find its boundaries, or go to its source? But of course you know all this! For you were born before it was all created, and you are so very experienced!"

(Job 38:1–21 TLB)

COUNTERFEIT OBEDIENCE ISN'T NEGOTIABLE

I could hand you my daughter's play money. The dollars look real, but down at the bottom it says "non-negotiable." You have enough sense to know that you're not going to be able to spend that money. It simply isn't negotiable—you can't make a deal with it.

> You can't change God's mind or outwit Him. He won't buy it.

But when it comes to the kingdom of God, you keep trying to take parts of His Word and make a counterfeit. That's the height of self-deception. You believe things that are contrary to God's law and try to get Him to negotiate a deal. He won't buy it. Not now, and not ever.

Somewhere in your own deception, you believe you can change God's mind or outwit Him. You keep tripping over the same things time and time again, simply because you refuse to settle the issue of obedience in your heart once and for all.

When you obey God's law, grace can come to you.

204

Don't Rob God

Tithing is non-negotiable. You cannot reason it away. God will not take pity on you and pour out His grace in spite of your stiff-necked refusal to obey Him.

"I'm not going to tithe," you say.

That is certainly your choice. God will never take away your right to choose. But you need to understand that grace will not abound to you. Don't get upset when your neighbors are walking around with every blessing of God being poured out on them. They simply settled the obedience issue in their own hearts. For some people it has come down to this: "If I die, I'll die obeying God with every fiber of my being."

The truth is, someday you will die, and you will face judgment before God.

Yes, woe upon you, Pharisees, and you other religious leaders—hypocrites! For you tithe down to the last mint leaf in your garden, but ignore the important things—justice and mercy and faith. Yes, you should tithe, but you shouldn't leave the more important things undone.

(Matthew 23:23 TLB)

God Won't Look the Other Way

Another non-negotiable item is sin.

"I just have a bad habit."

"I just have a problem."

I don't care what you call it. Sin is non-negotiable with God. He has paid a very high price for your salvation and, might I say, your obedience.

205

Sin must get out of your life.

"Pastor, what should I do about my sin?"

Quit.

From then on, Jesus began to preach, "Turn from sin and turn to God, for the Kingdom of Heaven is near."
(Matthew 4:17 TLB)

GOD FORGAVE YOU

The third non-negotiable element, if you want to achieve success in your personal and professional life, is forgiveness. God forgave you. Therefore, you have no excuse for any unforgiveness in your heart. When you settle this issue once and for all time, you're on your way to allowing grace to work in your life.

> God gives grace to His children; everyone else hopes for mercy.

Your heavenly Father will forgive you if you forgive those who sin against you; but if you refuse to forgive them, he will not forgive you.
(Matthew 6:14–15 TLB)

TAKE YOUR PLACE AS CHILDREN OF GOD

Grace only comes to children of God. The Bible says, *"But as many as received Him, to them He gave the right to become children of God"* (John 1:12).

When you take your place as a child of God, He will take His place as your Father. He only gives grace to His children; everyone else hopes for mercy.

We have a church full of people not taking their place as children of God. They are constantly crying for mercy when

206

what they need is grace. Mercy is a sovereign move of God. Grace is the birthright of His children.

As obedient children, not conforming yourselves to the former lusts, as in your ignorance; but as He who called you is holy, you also be holy in all your conduct, because it is written, "Be holy, for I am holy." (1 Peter 1:14–16)

In order for you to take your place as His children, you have to become holy. Once you get saved, you can't live like the world anymore. You are no longer of this world; God took you out. He delivered you from the kingdom and the power of darkness. He brought you into the kingdom of light—His dear children. You are no longer people of darkness; therefore, you are now called to walk in holiness.

Holiness is non-negotiable.

Looking for the blessed hope and glorious appearing of our great God and Savior Jesus Christ, who gave Himself for us, that He might redeem us from every lawless deed and purify for Himself His own special people, zealous for good works. (Titus 2:13–14)

LET YOUR WORDS BE FILLED WITH GRACE

If you want to live a holy lifestyle and experience the grace of God in your life, you're going to have to do something about your tongue. The Bible says that the tongue is an unruly evil. Out of the mouth you can bless God one moment and curse Him the next. That's why the first thing the Lord takes over when you're baptized with the Holy Spirit is your tongue.

You talk about your children.

You talk about your wife or husband.

You talk about your boss and coworkers.

You talk about your pastor.

You should not be saying the things that you are saying.

God is listening.

You are grieving the Holy Spirit and grace will not abound to you.

Keep your tongue from evil, and your lips from speaking deceit. (Psalm 34:13)

If you will dwell in holiness, you will find yourself living in the secret place of the Most High. You will abide under the shadow of the Almighty. (See Psalm 91:1–2.) You will be secure in God's strong tower. You will enjoy success and victory in the empowering presence of God.

CONFESSION:

Father, forgive me for disobedience. Reveal to me the ways that I've been deceived. Create a clean heart in me and allow me the grace to live in holiness before You, safe in the shelter of Your arms. Amen.

FAITH KEY #29— DON'T FRUSTRATE THE GRACE

Here are five ways to cooperate with God's grace:

Surrender—You must realize that God has called you and set you apart for His purposes, which means holiness.

Stop fighting it.

Surrender.

Submission—Accept the fact that you have a holy calling on your life. You can't keep running from God. Grace has the power to accomplish everything He's called you to do.

Yield—Yield to God, read His Word, and pray. Confessing the Word daily is a way to yield daily. Paul said, *"I die daily"* (1 Corinthians 15:31). Why does a dead man need the Word of God? That he might live again.

Resistance—You have to resist, but stop resisting God. This is where you start keeping yourself holy. Resist all situations that pull you away from holiness. Resist everything that pulls you away from your first love. Flee from it! If you resist evil, the empowering presence of God will cause it to flee from you. (See James 4:7.)

Choosing—Choose to listen to that still small voice of God on the inside of you throughout the day. Listen for Him. Stay attentive to Him. You will walk in holiness, and all grace will abound to you.

Do these things daily.

Make them a way of life.

Cast me not away from thy presence; and take not thy holy spirit from me. (Psalm 51:11 KJV)

Key #30

THE FAVOR OF GOD

The Favor of God Is the Keeping Power of God

I've spent a lot of time showing you that grace is not "unmerited favor," and I believe that you have a grasp on grace. Now that you have grace—the empowering presence of God—firmly in mind, I want you to see that there is a different blessing of God, which is His favor.

To understand favor, you need to see the difference between favor and grace.

Let me give you an example of favor. You were in a hurry to get to work and drove 75 mph in a 35 mph zone. You were wrong. There was a speed trap set up that you didn't see, and the policeman pulled you over. You were without excuse. You were speeding and he had proof. That's when you remembered that your car insurance expired and you never got around to renewing it. You are born again, Spirit-filled, and wrong. The policeman hauls you off to court. All you can do is repent because your fate is out of your hands now. You stand before the judge unjustified. You are without excuse.

Then, without any valid reason, the judge dismisses your case.

That's the favor of God.

You didn't deserve it, but the judge did you a favor.

Now let me give you an example of grace. You've been coming to church, hearing the Word of God, and obeying it. You are tithing. You are giving. You're meditating on the Word day and night.

At work you outshine everyone else. You're the first one in the door and the last one out. You produce more than anyone else in the company. You are clearly the best, and you know you're up for a promotion. There's only one problem. Your boss isn't a Christian and he really doesn't like you. He knows you've got the goods, but you're different from everyone else, and he doesn't like difference. There is no way he is going to recommend that you get promoted.

Then, all of a sudden, you get to work and find out that your boss has been reassigned to another location. Your new supervisor is a Christian and is mightily impressed with you. Not only does she recommend that you get the promotion, she orders that you get a raise.

What happened? God gave you what you were rightfully owed. Grace was bestowed upon you.

GOD FAVORED THE ISRAELITES

The book of Exodus tells how the children of Israel were in bondage to the Pharaoh of Egypt. He oppressed them cruelly, so God sent Moses to deliver them. At the hand of Moses, God sent many curses and plagues on the land, but Pharaoh still refused to let them go. When the time came for the last plague, God gave the Israelites favor with the Egyptians.

> *And the Lord gave the people favor in the sight of the Egyptians. Moreover the man Moses was very great in the land of Egypt, in the sight of Pharaoh's servants and in the sight of the people.* (Exodus 11:3)

So in the midst of the plagues, God gave the Israelites favor, and the favor of God caused the Israelites to leave Egypt with great wealth. The favor of God caused the Egyptians to give their money and jewels to the children of Israel. There is an important lesson to be learned from this. The children of Israel weren't seeking wealth. They sought God.

The same should be true in our lives. Don't seek money; seek the Lord.

When the favor of God comes upon you, it's too late for people who have done you wrong. If you mess with God's people, you've messed with God. Pharaoh did not get off easy. He'd been given plenty of chances, but when God rested His favor on Israel, He rested His judgment on their enemies.

> *For You, O Lord, will bless the righteous; with favor You will surround him as with a shield.* (Psalm 5:12)

God Favored Joseph

Whenever you read in the Bible that *"the Lord was with"* someone, it means that the favor of God rested upon them. In Genesis 39, we see that God was with Joseph while he was a prisoner in Egypt.

> *Now Joseph had been taken down to Egypt. And Potiphar, an officer of Pharaoh, captain of the guard, an Egyptian,*

bought him from the Ishmaelites who had taken him down there. The LORD was with Joseph, and he was a successful man; and he was in the house of his master the Egyptian.
(Genesis 39:1–2)

The Lord was with Joseph, and he prospered.

Wait a minute. He was a slave! He'd just been sold into slavery by his own brothers. He didn't have any money, so how could he have prospered?

He was prosperous because the favor of God was upon him. He didn't have anything but favor. He was rejected by his own brothers, and sent into slavery in a foreign land. Our problem is that we associate prosperity with money. Money is the lowest form of prosperity. Real prosperity is the favor of God.

> Money is the lowest form of prosperity. Real prosperity is the favor of God.

Favor can be seen by other people. Joseph's master saw something on him. He may not have known what it was, but the Bible says that his master saw that the Lord was with him.

And his master saw that the LORD was with him and that the LORD made all he did to prosper in his hand. So Joseph found favor in his sight, and served him. Then he made him overseer of his house, and all that he had he put under his authority.
(Genesis 39:3–4)

Joseph was in the pits, but the favor of God caused him to be promoted as overseer of the whole house. He had no money; his master had all the money. You may not have money. Your company may have it all, but the favor of God will bring the wealth of the wicked into your hand.

213

Let them shout for joy and be glad, who favor my righteous cause; and let them say continually, "Let the LORD be magnified, who has pleasure in the prosperity of His servant."
(Psalm 35:27)

GOD FAVORED ISAAC

Isaac was a very prosperous man. One year he received a one-hundredfold increase on all the seed he planted, but that's not what made him rich. He was prosperous because God favored him.

There was a famine in the land, besides the first famine that was in the days of Abraham. And Isaac went to Abimelech king of the Philistines, in Gerar. Then the LORD appeared to him and said: "Do not go down to Egypt; live in the land of which I shall tell you." (Genesis 26:1–2)

There was a great famine in the land, and Isaac was ready to get out of town with everybody else. But God said no. It didn't make a lick of sense. There was no food or water, yet God told him to stay put. The Lord basically said, "Let everybody else go. I want you to stay."

This is where most people get into trouble. They think they're smarter than God. Everybody knows you don't prosper if you stay put in the middle of a famine. But Isaac had already made up his mind that he would obey God. Even if it made no sense to him.

So Isaac waved good-bye to all his neighbors as they left for a better life. They shook their heads at his stupidity as they packed their camels.

Then Isaac sowed in that land, and reaped in the same year a hundredfold; and the LORD blessed him. The man began

214

to prosper, and continued prospering until he became very prosperous; for he had possessions of flocks and possessions of herds and a great number of servants. So the Philistines envied him.　　　　　　　　　　(Genesis 26:12–14)

If you are willing and obedient, the blessings of God will overtake you. That's exactly what happed to Isaac. God told him to stay put in the middle of a famine and Isaac was willing and obedient to God. In the middle of the famine, Isaac sowed his seed, and in one year he received one hundred times as much as he planted.

You don't have to fall victim to the famines around you either.

All you have to do is be willing and obedient to God.

The Bible says that we should not lean on our own understanding. (See Proverbs 3:5.) If Isaac had depended

> If you are willing and obedient, the blessings of God will overtake you.

on what he knew to do, he would have missed out on great wealth. If you are obedient to God, the blessings will come looking for you and overtake you. Obedience will bring you favor.

FELLOWSHIP BRINGS FAVOR

I have a problem with people who preach prosperity from God without fellowship, because it won't work. You cannot receive prosperity without holiness. You can't have holiness without being in fellowship with God.

Consider Isaac for a minute. Yes, he *obeyed* God. But first he *heard* God. That means he was in fellowship with God. He took time to hear what God had to say, and then he obeyed.

All the blessings of God come from fellowship. The whole Bible boils down to one thing: God wants a family. He wants relationships. He already has created beings; they're called angels. He doesn't want puppets; He wants you.

He wants to talk to you.

He expects you to listen.

When you do, He will be with you.

He'll cause you to live victoriously.

That's favor.

By this I know that You are well pleased with me, because my enemy does not triumph over me. (Psalm 41:11)

CONFESSION:

Father, it is the desire of my heart to be in constant fellowship with You. Forgive me for all the times that I have strayed, for the times I have avoided You, and for the times in which I let myself become to busy to become still and seek Your presence. When I do come to You, help me to remember to listen as much as I speak. Then, Lord, give me the strength to obey. Amen.

FAITH KEY #30—THE FAVOR OF GOD

The Bible says that Jesus increased in favor with God and man. (See Luke 2:52.) If you haven't already figured it out, whatever God did for Jesus, He will do for you. The Lord's desire is that you live a life of personal and professional success, with nothing missing and nothing broken. He desires to release His grace—His empowering presence—to cause you to become everything that He has called you to be and to do everything He has asked you to do.

Favor is the icing on the cake.

On top of everything else He's done, God will place His favor upon you.

He will be with you.

He will make you the best at whatever He has called you to do.

He will fight your battles.

He will bring you prosperity.

Because of His favor, you'll find faith to be the best.

May God's peace, grace, and favor rest upon you today and every day of your life, and may you have no missing links in your victorious living.

—*Pastor Lamont McLean*

About the Author

Lamont McLean lives his life beyond limitations. Born with a speech impediment, he accepted detentions rather than give oral reports in school. He avoided social situations and withdrew from other people. As a computer programmer, he was passed over for promotions and told that he was "not management material."

In 1985, however, God told Lamont, "I'm calling you to raise up a church. You'll do it with your own finances, because I'll teach you how to run My business by showing you how to run your own."

Today, Lamont McLean owns an international technology company with over one hundred thirty employees.

He pastors Living Faith Christian Center, a flourishing church of more than six thousand, located in Pennsauken, New Jersey.

He is dynamic, compassionate, and steadfast as he teaches the word of faith through the uncompromising Word of God. His teachings have been circulated throughout the world through his numerous audio and video series.

10 Curses That Block the Blessing
Larry Huch

Have you been suffering with depression, family dysfunction, marital unhappiness, or other problems and been unable to overcome them? Within the pages of this groundbreaking book, *10 Curses That Block the Blessing,* Larry Huch shares his personal experience with a life of anger, drug addiction, crime, and violence. He shows how he broke these curses and reveals how you can recognize the signs of a curse, be set free from generational curses, and restore your health and wealth. You don't have to struggle any longer. Choose to revolutionize your life. You can reverse the curses that block your blessings!

ISBN: 978-0-88368-207-4 • Trade • 272 pages

www.whitakerhouse.com

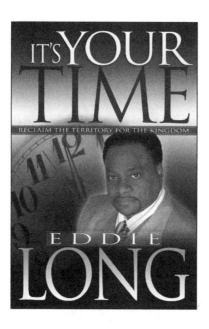

It's Your Time:
Reclaim Your Territory for the Kingdom
Eddie Long

Have we, as believers, allowed the world to silence us? By slowly eroding our rights to free speech…by passing laws saying that marriage isn't necessarily between a man and a woman…that murder is okay… that it's wrong to display the Ten Commandments… Is this really equality for all, except for Christians?

Join Eddie Long in reclaiming what has been lost. He will inspire you to rise up, take authority, and boldly assert your power as a believer. Discover how to redefine your life's purpose and vision while you raise your children to be godly leaders. Speak up, Christians! Now is the time for our unified voice to be heard, to take a stand together, and to stand firm. It's our time.

ISBN: 978-0-88368-783-3 • Hardcover • 192 pages

WHITAKER
HOUSE

www.whitakerhouse.com

The Principles and Power of Vision
Dr. Myles Munroe

Whether you are a businessperson, a homemaker, a student, or a head of state, best-selling author Dr. Myles Munroe explains how you can make your dreams and hopes a living reality. Your success is not dependent on the state of the economy or what the job market is like. You do not need to be hindered by the limited perceptions of others or by a lack of resources. Discover time-tested principles that will enable you to fulfill your vision no matter who you are or where you come from.

You were not meant for a mundane or mediocre life.
Revive your passion for living, pursue your dream,
discover your vision—and find your true life.

ISBN: 978-0-88368-951-6 • Hardcover • 240 pages

WHITAKER
HOUSE

www.whitakerhouse.com

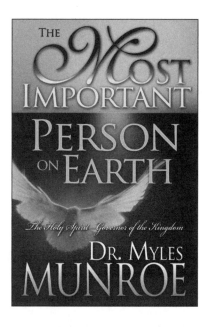

The Most Important Person on Earth:
The Holy Spirit, Governor of the Kingdom

Dr. Myles Munroe

In *The Most Important Person on Earth*, Dr. Myles Munroe explains how the Holy Spirit is the Governor of God's kingdom on earth, much as royal governors administered the will of earthly kings in their territories. Under the guidance and enabling of the Holy Spirit, you will discover how to bring order to the chaos in your life, receive God's power to heal and deliver, fulfill your true purpose with joy, become a leader in your sphere of influence, and be part of God's government on earth. Enter into the fullness of God's Spirit as you embrace God's design for your life today.

ISBN: 978-0-88368-986-8 • Hardcover • 320 pages

www.whitakerhouse.com

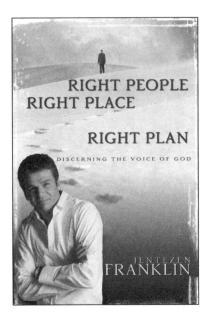

**Right People, Right Place, Right Plan:
Discerning the Voice of God**
Jentezen Franklin

Whom should I marry? What will I do with my life?
Do I take this job? Should I invest money in this opportunity?

God has bestowed an incredible gift in the heart of every believer.
He has given you an internal compass to help guide your life, your
family, your children, your finances, and much more. Jentezen Franklin
reveals how, through the Holy Spirit, you can tap into the heart
and mind of the Almighty. Learn to trust those divine "nudges" and
separate God's voice from all other voices in your life. Tap into your
supernatural gift of spiritual discernment and you will better be able
to fulfill your purpose as a child of God.

ISBN: 978-0-88368-276-0 • Hardcover • 208 pages

www.whitakerhouse.com